WOMEN IN BUSINESS

WOMEN IN BUSINESS

The Changing Face of Leadership

Patricia Werhane, Margaret Posig, Lisa Gundry,
Laurel Ofstein, and Elizabeth Powell

Foreword by Margaret Heffernan

PRAEGER

Westport, Connecticut
London

Library of Congress Cataloging-in-Publication Data

Women in business : the changing face of leadership / Patricia Werhane... [et al.] ; foreword
    by Margaret Heffernan.
        p. cm.
    Includes bibliographical references and index.
    ISBN 978–0–275–99454–9 (alk. paper)
1. Women executives—Case studies. 2. Women in development—Case studies. 3. Sex role in
the work environment—Case studies. I. Werhane, Patricia Hogue.
HD6054.3.W636 2007
658.4′092082—dc22   2007028636

British Library Cataloguing in Publication Data is available.

Library of Congress Catalog Card Number: 2007028636
ISBN-13: 978–0–275–99454–9

First published in 2007

Praeger Publishers, 88 Post Road West, Westport, CT 06881
An imprint of Greenwood Publishing Group, Inc.
www.praeger.com

Printed in the United States of America

The paper used in this book complies with the
Permanent Paper Standard issued by the National
Information Standards Organization (Z39.48–1984).

10 9 8 7 6 5 4 3 2 1

For my four daughters: Hillary, Kelly, Marijke, and Stephanie.
  —Patricia Werhane

For my family...Bill, Katie, and Luke...and my parents, who have been so support-ive of my career.
  And for all of the women who are constantly trying to achieve the best balance between work and family.
  —Margaret Posig

For Anny: always curious, always courageous, always present.
  —Lisa Gundry

For the women who told me their stories and for the women leaders of the future.
  —Laurel Ofstein

For my husband, Kirby Hutto.
  —Elizabeth Powell

Contents

Foreword

The women in this book, the women who wrote it, and most of the women who read it all grew up in a male-dominated world. In our lifetime, men have been running the companies and the countries. True, there have been a few female heads of states—Margaret Thatcher and Golda Meir spring most readily to mind. But, for the most part, power and leadership have assumed a monotonously male face.

But that is starting to change. At time of writing, eighteen countries are governed by women—and, of these, only three women were born to their role. For the first time ever, Germany has a female Head of State, and both the United States and France have seen a viable, female candidate for the Presidency. For decades now, women have begun to infiltrate the executive suites and boardrooms of corporate America. Today some 14.6 percent of board seats are held by women, 15.6 percent of corporate officers are women, and 6.7 percent of the top earners in America are women. These numbers are nowhere near good enough and the progression is not steady; most of these 2006 numbers are down from 2005 and, at that rate of progress, it will take 73 years for women to achieve parity with men. But what is important is that there are fewer and fewer firsts: every time a woman inhabits a position of power, it looks more and more normal.

Outside the realms of government and for the *Fortune* 500, progress has been faster. Nearly half the private companies in the United States today are owned or controlled by women. Their 10.4 million businesses employ more people than the *Fortune* 500 *combined*. And these companies are not all making handbags and cookies; they are vibrant contributors to every sector of the world's greatest economy. Indeed, there are those who argued that America's narrow escape from recession in 2002 could be attributed entirely to the growth in women-owned businesses.

These numbers are important not just in and of themselves. Numbers matter because the more women there are in business, the freer those women can feel to be themselves. Alone, a woman at the top of an organization is under immense pressure to assimilate to male norms; we have all seen this happen. But, surrounded by other women, mentored by them, and mentoring them, remaining true to oneself becomes a great deal easier. And so the accumulation of women, in positions of power, does something that everyone recognizes but hesitates to acknowledge: It changes the norm.

When I studied the rise of female entrepreneurship in my book *How She Does It*, what struck me most forcibly was not just that women were everywhere—in oil and gas, electricity, high tech, biotech, wholesale, retail, construction, and robotics. What struck me most was that their companies didn't feel the same as other companies I'd known, run by men and employing, mostly, men. As I interviewed hundreds of women business owners, a distinct pattern began to emerge. These leaders were not emulating a military command-and-control style of leadership; they did not think they knew all the answers and they did not believe they were solely responsible for their companies' success. They did business plans but they were also gifted improvisers, more focused on improving the future than correcting the past. They placed values at the center of their businesses and they clung to those values through thick and thin. Immense attention and enormous resources were poured into building healthy, vibrant company cultures. Mistakes were regarded as learning and passion was seen, not as a weakness but as a strength. Asking for help was respected, since every business needs more intelligence than any one person can provide.

These characteristics cropped up time and time again, no matter the age, industry, or location of the business. Yet still I struggled to put my finger on why these companies just felt so different. In the end, I have come to believe that their success stems from a very particular mindset: one that sees companies not as machines but as living organisms. What is the test of a healthy organism? That it can sustain itself. And that it can sustain others.

When sustainability is the goal and test of leadership, the nature of leadership changes. And when you have enough leaders who understand this, and enact it, the norms change too. Any one of the women in this book would be interesting enough on her own. What makes all of them so exciting is that, together, they are redefining what we mean by leadership and what we mean by success. I believe that this change is more profound and more transformative than anything our generation has seen.

That isn't to say that the triumph of this form of leadership is assured. Far from it. But we can see today that these are inspiring ways to work and to lead. We can see that values don't have to be a trade-off for profits and that humanity is central, not peripheral, to growing a business. We can see leaders like those in this book, proving not just their own worth but the value of their values every day. And my hunch is that, when such women have finally, successfully, redefined the male business norms we all grew up with, we will be left asking: What took you so long?

Margaret Heffernan

Author, *How She Does It: How Women Entrepreneurs Are Changing the Rules of Business Success*

Acknowledgments

We gratefully acknowledge a number of people who have made this book possible. The book was the brainstorm of Donni Case, former president of Financial Relations Board and a longtime member of The Chicago Network. With her help we were able to successfully contact and interview many women who are members of the Network, a Chicago organization for women who are leaders in their organizations or who have national visibility. The Network and the wonderful women who are members were key to the success of this project, and we thank this organization and its Executive Director, Amy Osler, profusely. The development of this book is a result, and many of the chapters are stories of Network women. Robert Harris, then Dean of the Darden School at the University of Virginia, provided us contacts with Madeleine Ludlow and Beth Pritchard. Special thanks to Jill Kickul, Forsythe Chair in Entrepreneurship at Miami University of Ohio, for her support and introducing us to Margaret Heffernan, who kindly agreed to write the Foreword of this book.

A *very* short version of the book first appeared as Chapter One of Margaret Foegen Karsten's three-volume collection, *Gender, Race, and Ethnicity in the Workplace,* published by Praeger. That chapter could not have been possible without the interviewing and writing assistance of Jane Carlson. Nicholas Philipson, then senior editor at Praeger, encouraged us to develop our ideas into a book.

Most of the interviews and the organization of the book were due to the work of Laurel Ofstein, Assistant Director of the Leo V. Ryan Center for Creativity and Innovation at DePaul University. We also thank Ewelina Ignasia for her assistance with the content analysis of the interview data. Other invaluable assistance was provided by Jenny Mead and Summer Brown. The book could not be possible without the support of The Institute for

Business and Professional Ethics at DePaul University and the Darden School at the University of Virginia.

Patricia Werhane
Margaret Posig
Lisa Gundry
Laurel Ofstein
Elizabeth Powell

Introduction

Women have made enormous strides in recent decades, as they entered and rose through the ranks of corporations to attain leadership positions. Despite these gains, however, and despite the number of women in business schools, and in lower and middle management positions, the status of women at the top of corporate America has not increased as expected. According to the 2006 Census released by Catalyst, a research and advisory organization that conducts research on women's career advancement, in 2006 women held just 15.6% of Fortune 500 corporate officer positions, fewer than the previous year (16.4% in 2005). Catalyst also reported that the number of companies with three or more women corporate officers decreased as well in 2006. On the positive side, the number of women in top-paying positions increased to 6.7%, up from 6.4% in 2005 (Catalyst 2007).

As of 2006, there were only eight women who were CEOs of a Fortune 500 company, and only 14.6% of the Fortune 500 board seats were held by women. On average, women earned 76 cents for every dollar earned by men (Urban Institute 2004). There are only 87 women in the U.S. Congress (out of 535 seats), and so far no woman has been elected president of the United States. According to the Institute for Women's Policy Research:

> Women have made tremendous progress toward gaining economic equality during the last several decades. Nonetheless, throughout the United States, women earn less, are less likely to own a business, and are more likely to live in poverty than men. Disparities abound regionally and by state, and, even more profoundly, race and ethnicity continue to shape women's economic opportunities.
>
> (Caiazza, Shaw, and Werschkul 2004, 4)

Despite these daunting statistics, women are making inroads and becoming more influential in leadership positions in corporate America. This book is a celebration of twenty-two of these women, their achievements, the values and visions they bring to and enact in their organizations, and the contributions they have made to the companies in which they hold leadership positions.

OUR STUDY OF WOMEN LEADERS

Some of the women leaders interviewed for this book have started from the bottom of an organization; others have moved from one organization to another; still others have started their own businesses. Included in our study are women in finance, manufacturing, labor, banking, accounting, consulting, architecture and design, real estate, energy, marketing, and health care. Our aim is to do more than celebrate the achievements of these women. We searched for common leadership development lessons that could serve as models for women now entering, progressing, and leading in the workplace. Although we have selected women in a variety of sectors of the economy, several underlying themes emerged that suggested distinct preferences for certain styles of leadership as well as norms and values reinforced by these leaders to shape, and in some cases change, their organizations.

Each of the women we have chosen to profile has a different story to tell. The narratives they weave tell us both something about themselves and more importantly about what they value and how they demonstrate and communicate those values to those with whom they work. Unlike leaders in hierarchically structured organizations, these women do not view their authority as a matter of power. These women are not transactional leaders who view leadership as a series of transactions between managers and employees or a trade of promotion or a salary for performance. They often see themselves as team leaders, as inspirational rather than directive. Many of these women see themselves as working to coordinate and balance their interests and those of their employees, transforming these into shared corporate goals. This is usually translated into forms of interactive and participatory leadership that empowers employees while achieving corporate ends. This style of leadership is not merely aimed at transforming employees to adapt the values and goals of the company. Rather, leadership is thought of as a two-way interaction where both managers and employees are motivated and sometimes even changed (Couto 1994, 102–7). So the leadership style is more like coaching than directing, more participative than hierarchical.

Despite various struggles and challenges and even discriminatory treatment, the women found ways to overcome these obstacles. Mentoring experiences, both positive and negative, were very influential to their own leadership development. They also repeatedly speak of the importance of mentoring others. Many have worked in hierarchical organizations where

they were ignored. Yet these women emphasize the importance of collaboration, of listening, and of inclusion in decision-making.

To what is the leadership success of these women attributable? Is their
success contingent on circumstances, so that, in other circumstances they
would not have had opportunities, or, given their talents, they could not succeed in other industries or under other market conditions? Of course, the
context in which one finds oneself plays a critical role in one's ability to succeed or fail. And there is always a bit of luck involved. Anne Arvia's
appointment as President of ShoreBank, for example, was due to the death
of her mentor. Had Eva Maddox not come into contact with Stanley Tigerman, world-renowned architect and designer, her creative path would have
been quite different. But these women and the others we have studied also
demonstrate the ability to make the most of their talents given the situations
in which they find themselves and many demonstrate the ability to redefine
that context.

Communication as well as collaboration—communicating to and with
managers and employees—is another theme running through these chapters. Transparency, defined as honest and open communication, and sharing
information are emphasized repeatedly. While some of these women have
been passed over for executive positions in the past, we find that many
emphasized the importance of hiring, promoting, and including the most
talented managers and employees without fear of being second-guessed,
sharing power, or being replaced.

Throughout the stories profiled in this book, women speak of the ways in
which they influence their organizations through an inclusive style—
empowering their employees as colleagues rather than as subordinates or
followers. Indeed, the words "subordinate" and "follower" seldom surfaced in the interviews we conducted, demonstrating a perspective of egali-
tarian as opposed to hierarchical relationships.

Many of these women have found themselves in difficult economic situations either because the company they are leading has experienced tough
economic times during the post–2001 period, for example, or because they
found themselves in a leadership position in an organization that had not
been led well in the past. Rather than becoming discouraged, some of the
women we interviewed saw these problems as challenges, and became
change agents and attacked them with enthusiasm and intelligence. Other
women leaders have experienced different challenges in their organizations.
For example, some women are restless with the status quo and have
embarked on a quest for excellence.

Each of the women profiled in this book was carefully chosen because of
the leadership position she had successfully attained in her organization or
in multiple organizations. This book presents an in-depth study of twenty-
two women leaders across a wide range of industries, backgrounds, and
positions. Our approach is to provide a rich set of portraits of these women
leaders, as well as a content analysis of the themes and issues uncovered in
the interviews on which the chapters are based. In the concluding chapter

we present a summary of what these women leaders we studied can teach us about leadership in business.

This book is unique not only in the profiles of the subjects studied but in the timeliness—indeed, urgency—of its coverage of such themes as business ethics, social responsibility, and the need for innovation and change that emerge in many of the chapters. The lessons of this book are of great interest to management teams and organizations around the world that are trying to create and sustain leadership that is reflective of the needs and concerns of the stakeholders and communities they serve. As the stories of these women unfold, we remember the words of Margaret Mead:

> *Never doubt that a small group of thoughtful, committed citizens can change the world. Indeed, it is the only thing that ever has.*

REFERENCES

Caiazza, A., A. Shaw, and M. Werschkul. 2004. *Women's economic status in the States: Wide disparities by race, ethnicity, and region.* Washington, DC: Institute for Women's Policy Research.

Catalyst. 2007. 2006 Census of Women Corporate Officers, Top Earners, and Directors of the Fortune 500. http://www.catalyst.org/pressroom/press_releases/2006_Census_Release.pdf (accessed March 17, 2007).

Couto, Richard A. 1994. The transformation of transforming leadership. In *Leader's companion,* ed. J. Thomas Wren. New York: Free Press.

Urban Institute. 2004. Unpublished calculations for the Institute for Women's Policy Research based on the U.S. Bureau of the Census Public Use Microdata Sample, 2000.

Chapter 1

Founding and Growing the Values-Based Enterprise: Phyllis Apelbaum

My desire was to earn a decent living to support my son and to be the master of my own fate. I wasn't looking for power. I was looking to earn a living.

ENTREPRENEURIAL LEADERSHIP: THE EMERGENCE AND GROWTH OF WOMEN-OWNED BUSINESSES

Women have launched entrepreneurial careers in record numbers during the past two decades. The emergence and growth of women-owned businesses have contributed strongly to the global economy and to their surrounding communities. The routes women have followed to take leadership roles in business are varied; yet, more likely than not, most women business owners have overcome or worked to avoid obstacles and challenges in creating their businesses. The presence of women in the workplace driving small and entrepreneurial organizations has had a tremendous impact on employment and on the culture of the workplace.

According to the Center for Women's Business Research, as of 2006 there were an estimated 10.4 million firms headed by women. Moreover, for the past two decades, majority women-owned (51% or more) firms grew at twice the rate of all firms. Further, women-owned firms employed 12.8 million people and generated $1.9 trillion in sales (Center for Women's Business Research 2007).

Founding their own businesses enables women to use, satisfy, and maintain high levels of skill, as perhaps they could not when working for a corporation (Alvarez and Meyer 1998). Women also cite layoffs, the ability to make one's own decisions, and the need for more flexible working hours to accommodate family demands as reasons for starting their own businesses. Having young children was a strong positive influence on

Phyllis Apelbaum

women's self-selection of entrepreneurship (Boden 1996). Still additional motivation comes from the belief that the world can be different and that their businesses can provide a means to change things and make a difference for other women (Gundry and Ben-Yoseph 2003).

BIRTH OF A BUSINESS: THE LAUNCH OF ARROW MESSENGER SERVICE, INC.

Among successful entrepreneurs, it is often difficult to separate the entrepreneur from the business. If there is anyone who lives, breathes, and sleeps her job, it is Phyllis Apelbaum. As President and CEO of Arrow Messenger Service, Inc. in Chicago, IL, she positively loves what she does for a living. Arrow Messenger Service is a full-service delivery and facility company, with revenues of over $8 million per year. The firm was founded in 1974.

One of the primary characteristics of entrepreneurial leaders is the passion that drives them. This passion is demonstrated by their perseverance in the face of adversity, the extraordinary initiative they take to accomplish challenging goals, and their strong need to achieve success while at the same time having a low need for status and power.

Apelbaum's aspiration was never power or influence. Her greatest desire was simply to earn a good living in order to provide for her son, and at the same time, to be the master of her own time, and ultimately master of her own fate. Having finished school at eighth grade, her lack of a college education definitely shaped her future experiences. Apelbaum has indeed made a huge success of that initial desire. She has remained the master of her own domain by leading Arrow Messenger Service, Inc. for thirty-three years and counting.

One of the strongest influences on Apelbaum's entrepreneurial path was when her father passed away in 1973. At that time, Apelbaum was working for City Bonded Messenger Service, a messenger company in Chicago, where she had been employed for fourteen years. The ownership of the company had just been changed, and the subsequent changes in the firm's culture and people did not suit her. She was contemplating moving on.

I was a single parent raising a child. My dad died suddenly, very suddenly, at the age of 56. When I went to California to bury him and close his house and do the things you do when you lose a parent, it became very clear that he had died without fulfilling one of his greatest desires. He was a working man who wanted to go to Hawaii. He had a bank bottle in his bedroom, one of those little Seagram's Seven bottles, and on it was a tape that said, "Hawaii bound." In 1973, it cost fifty-nine dollars to go to Hawaii. I remember sitting on the floor thinking, how does a person live and die, raise a family, and not get from LA to Hawaii for fifty-nine dollars? And so, coming home on the airplane it was kind of like, this just isn't going to happen to me—not more, not less.

Right before my dad's death in June of that year, the company [City Bonded] was sold. I had new employers and I wasn't really happy about the change. Whenever there's a massive change like that, people are different and so the environment is different. I had worked for a couple that were warm and caring and inclusive, and now I was working for somebody who was totally different, and then a month after that my dad dies suddenly.

I decided I would go on and do something else. So I gave my notice and said that I would work until November 1st of 1974. What happened during that period of time was my competitors—the people who were my competitors then and some who are today—would call and say, "oh, have we got a job for you, boy have we got a job for you," offering me more money than I could have imagined. And then, one night I was talking to a friend and that person said, "Could you imagine if you're worth that much to them what you could be worth to yourself?" And I said, "You know, that's a real possibility."

After the death of my father, the couple who originally had owned City Bonded came to visit, the Mansfields (Irving and Nadine). They came to pay a condolence call, and I told Irving about the whole situation and what was going on. He said, "Why don't you just do it for yourself?" I said, I was kind of thinking about that but, not so sure I could. He said, "Of course you could, you did it for me." So I decided to take my inheritance, which by the way was $3,500, and I decided that I would use that to get my license and to get started. The truth is I had seventeen hearings and did not get my license, simply because the Commerce Commission had never given a license to a woman—not for any other reason...until I met the man who's in that picture right there [pointing to a framed picture on the wall of her office]—he was then the Chief Hearing Officer for the Commerce Commission. Today he's the

Illinois Supreme Justice for the State of Illinois, Charles Freeman. He was the Commissioner when I met him.

I lost, I lost my $3,500; I lost my opportunity to get my license; I lost my opportunity to become the master of my own fate; and, at the end of the day I just went barging into his office. He says that I sounded like I sold fish for a living on Maxwell Street. So I told Charles the story of what happened and he corrected it. He saw to it that I got my license and became a mentor and a friend, and really my entrée into the political world. I didn't have any political involvement before that. That picture there is [former Chicago mayor] Harold Washington's inauguration, and it was through Charles that I got involved in all of that. And thus began the birth of Arrow Messenger Service. I opened up the doors on November 1st, 1974 and went to work.

OVERCOMING OBSTACLES: THE ENTREPRENEURIAL CHALLENGE

Access to capital has been a significant business concern of women entrepreneurs during the past two decades. Until quite recently, the primary capital sources available to women were personal savings, including credit cards, and loans from family and friends that they used to finance their new ventures. Apelbaum concurred that one of the biggest hurdles she faced in founding her business was capital. She had no line of credit or access to capital. Her first "line of credit" was the result of a promise she made to a friend at a local bank. Apelbaum told her friend that although the business was open and running, she had no money to handle the current cash flow situation. She bargained that if he would make sure that none of her checks bounced, she would put every penny that Arrow Messenger Service earned in his bank. He believed in her and agreed to help. Apelbaum kept her promise and banked exclusively with this bank until it closed several years later.

Just when Arrow Messenger Service was growing and burgeoning, Apelbaum was diagnosed with breast cancer. Now, over eleven years since she learned that the cancer had been eradicated, it has been another obstacle to overcome. Fortunately, the son that she had worked so hard to provide for, stepped up to the plate. Mark Apelbaum took over the leadership of Arrow Messenger Service during this difficult time and made sure that the company was running smoothly. Apelbaum said that this was a good learning experience for her: *I was hospitalized [for the cancer] and Mark took over. During this time I learned that the people around me were really good students and that I didn't need to be there 24/7.*

Apelbaum clearly enjoys people and is very much a people person. Throughout her life she made friends easily with people, including those on whom she eventually patterned herself.

My mom was a woman who had great strength. She was warm and caring and survived a lot of very tough things in her life, a lot of tough things. So her gift was one of survival. I had an aunt, Pepie Reiner—my mother's brother's wife (she was not a blood aunt) who was another big role model in my life. The purpose that she served was really more of a domestic role model. My mother was always a worker—always out trying to earn a living for our family. My aunt was always a homemaker, and so she's the one who taught me how to take care of myself, and how to clean the toilet, and the things that we learn that we have to do whether we like them or not. In the 8th grade, I had a particular teacher. Valia Pappas was her name. I always think of her very fondly. She was very kind, and she was supportive of my life and things that were going on in my life at that time. So she was another person who helped along the way. I've been very fortunate that in every decade of my life there have been different people for different reasons, and they just continue to come, and then I try today in some way to pay that back by offering it where I can.

Mentors and role models are the same to Apelbaum. She feels that people who are role models are the people you most want to be like. While Irving Mansfield was not someone she particularly wanted to copy, she certainly wanted to emulate his business model and follow his example. Apelbaum does consider herself a mentor. Obsessive about her work, she is anxious to point out that there is little balance between home and work when you are running a company. However, with thirty-three years of business ownership behind her, Apelbaum has discovered that it is OK to get away when you have been a good teacher. Her son recently led the company while Apelbaum vacationed in Arizona for three months and Apelbaum reports, *When I came back, everything was fine!*

A large part of Arrow Messenger Service's success can be attributed to Apelbaum's philosophy and values that she has developed into a culture emphasizing people and service. This is largely why, in Apelbaum's view, the company has survived over thirty years. In that time, she has seen massive changes in technology and business practices in general and she is proud to say that there aren't many small businesses in this industry which have survived for over three decades.

BUILDING AN EMPLOYEE-CENTERED CULTURE TO ACHIEVE THE CUSTOMER SERVICE MISSION

The preferred management styles of women entrepreneurs may be associated with their motives for business ownership. The results of a multi-case study on rural small business owners (Robinson 2001) indicated that women entrepreneurs were concerned about relationships with their employees and with creating corporate cultures that minimized interpersonal conflict. These preferences were consistent with their motives for starting their businesses. Researchers have described the relational practices engaged in by women entrepreneurs, which included collaborative decision-making within an empowered team atmosphere (Buttner 2001).

Apelbaum described the culture she has built over the past three decades:

We have people who have been here for a long time—both inside and outside. We provide an environment where people understand our role, our mission, and what we're really about. We have over two hundred people out there providing quality service, so our job internally is to bring the food home to those over two hundred people. So the accomplishment is—it's kind of like a chess game, if you will. When you play chess, at the end of the game—win or lose—the game is over. At the end of the day—win or lose—our day is over. Tomorrow morning at six o'clock, we just get started with a brand new day, and new pieces, and we keep doing that. Over thirty years—three hundred and sixty-five times thirty-three years is a lot of days to do that. A million deliveries a year is a lot of deliveries to do for over thirty years. Of course it wasn't always a million deliveries for thirty years, it grew as it went.

The accomplishment of just being here, providing an environment that allows people to understand that the quest here is to feed this small army. If we have two hundred people that we can feed today, that's great. If we have three hundred next year, that would be better. And so people who want to feel energized by that mission is really what it takes. When I think about the people who are here the longest, in particular I'm thinking about Tom Krier, he's our Controller (in a bigger company he'd be the CFO, in a little company you're the Controller). He came out of a very big environment. He came out of places like Abbott Labs and Baxter Labs. So what keeps him here? He says it is the variety of being part and parcel of everything that's going on. It's not such a big environment that your job is simply to count the beans. His role is really to be part and parcel of the management team.

I would say that, especially at this stage of the game, it's a really great thing that while we all work together as a team, they're very self-sufficient when I'm not here. They don't need me to be here to do their job. It's a really great thing that at this stage of the game, they know what their job is and they move it along, and it's very clear that they can do a good job at that. So that then allows me the opportunity to do lots of other things. That's a real gift—to be able to then spend some time giving back to the community some of what you take out of it.

Apelbaum makes a point to give back both to the community and to her industry. She defines her community service activities as those in which *you give of yourself and expect nothing in return.* She has served for over ten years on the Chicago Police Department Board. She also serves on the boards of the Rehabilitation Institute of Chicago and Meals on Wheels. In addition to giving back to the community, she uses her position as a force in her industry to organize others to achieve mutual goals. For example, she was the first female president of the Messenger Courier Companies of the Americas (MCCA). As the cofounder of the local association, Messenger Service Association of Illinois (MSAI), she worked with the Chicagoland Chamber of Commerce to have many downtown parking spaces specifically allocated for delivery parking.

Entrepreneurs tend to be very closely connected to the communities in which they do business, and many in fact do volunteer their time to nonprofit organizations, industry trade associations, and civic groups. Apelbaum firmly believes in giving people a break, and there are many individuals working at Arrow Messenger Service who never had the chance of a decent education, but nevertheless have proved themselves over the years and grown with the company. Other people use Arrow Messenger Service as a stepping-stone to other careers. Loyalty, too, is essential to her. A large number of her staff, numbering over 200, has been with her for many years. Her staff is clearly energized by the fact that there is a great deal of variety to the business—no two days are ever the same.

LEADERSHIP VALUES AND ETHICS IN THE GROWING NEW VENTURE

The business ethos at Arrow Messenger Service hinges on Apelbaum's personal values of equality and fairness. She has always maintained that it is essential to be fair and equal to all people, regardless of who they are. She practices what she preaches and has the following sign on her door: Say what you are going to do and do what you say, and do nothing less. Apelbaum treats everyone with respect and courtesy and has created a culture in which nothing short of that is tolerated. She explains:

> *Fairness, equality, rights—people's right to do what they want to do and how they want to do it. It's really important. If I want that for myself, then I should expect to extend that to you. I don't want anybody here—I don't allow anybody here—to be treated in a manner that's less than how they should be treated. I want everyone to give the customer one hundred percent. Don't charge them for one hundred percent and give them eighty. That's clearly not an okay thing to do. So the values of the organization are really not that different from my own.*

Communication is also the key in a business where customer service is paramount. Apelbaum is the first to admit that she is very demanding and expects 100% most of the time. Being a realist, she understands that this is almost impossible to achieve but it doesn't stop her striving for it. She is intent on providing the best possible messenger service in Chicago and constantly works on ways to identify and develop new opportunities to help achieve that. It is an absolute prerequisite that everyone who works at Arrow Messenger Service has to have this vision. It is a constant challenge leading people, finding the right hires, and socializing them to the firm's values.

Apelbaum's management style can be described as participative, as her employees are highly involved and empowered to make day-to-day decisions in their work.

I no longer spend my day walking around behind people making sure of what they're doing. If I need to do that over thirty years down the road, something's really, really wrong. I need to spend my time strategically. I need to do that more in meeting with the executive team and hearing how things are going. My role now is to help the executive team by asking them, "What can I do to help you?" What are their problems and what are the issues? What is it that we want to work on this year? Now we are on track to develop and grow the facility division of our business, as well as moving things in "brown boxes."

The integrity of a company is based on the integration of the firm's values into its driving systems. Entrepreneurs' guiding values should be clearly articulated, as Apelbaum has demonstrated in the strong connection her employees make to the mission of Arrow Messenger Service. Entrepreneurs also need to be willing to take action on the values they espouse, and the venture's system and structure must support and reinforce these values (Paine 1994). Entrepreneurs often face ethical dilemmas involving, for example, conflict of interest, personality traits, responsibility to stake-holders, and level of openness (Vyakarnam et al. 1997).

What ethical dilemmas has Apelbaum encountered?

We have, on a couple of occasions, turned down significant business because of ethical judgments. We walked away two years ago from a very big piece of business because we refused to work for the kind of person that was giving us that business. I got my license to go into this business because of [Charles Freeman's] ethics. He knew that it was absolutely wrong to have gone through the hearings that we did and not come out with a license. So his ethics were of such high value that there was no way he was going to let that happen under his watch.

I've walked away from people who have walked in the door and said, "If you hire me, I can bring these four accounts with me and I can bring $100,000 to the table easily." I clearly know that if they would do that coming here, they would do that leaving here. That's not in any way some one with whom I would want to deal.

On a similar note, an interesting situation occurred about fifteen years ago. A lawyer came to town and introduced the idea to her of using independent contractors rather than paid employees. By doing this, more money could be made by the company. Apelbaum didn't think it could work and refused to do it because she felt it was unethical. She recalls feeling that,

I wouldn't be able to sleep at night and it'll never work. Well, it has worked for fifteen years for other companies. Because of that ethical decision, we have not grown to be the biggest company in the city. We've grown nicely, no question about it, but we battle everyday—the company that has independent contractors and us, that has employees. Because if you have employees, you've *got about a 28% bottom number there. So if the two of us walk in the door and he charges you $1.00, I have to charge you $1.28. I'm always fighting that. The ethical decision to go in that direction meant we had to work harder at our vision to provide better service. Otherwise, why should you be willing to pay me 28 cents more? Why? There'd be no reason for it. How many people in the business community do you think really care that ethically we felt that this was the right thing to do for our drivers? Very few do.*

Apelbaum took her views to the political arena and argued for years to legislators. In 2004, a bill was ratified by the Illinois legislature to put firms with independent contractors and those with employees on an equal footing—but it took nearly nine years to do it.

One of the growing pains entrepreneurs face involves an ethical dilemma: should the venture accept a client or contract for which it may not be able to fulfill its promises?

Arrow Messenger Service had only been in business a few years when it received the opportunity of a lifetime. A company Apelbaum knew well was setting up package pickups nationwide and she was approached to be the Chicago vendor with a contract worth $500,000. That was a lot of money and Arrow Messenger Service was still a start-up. She agonized over how she could make it work but quickly realized that, at the time, the company was simply too small to take on the business. She went back to the company and said that, while she appreciated the opportunity, Arrow Messenger Service was not the right vendor for them. It was one of her most painful decisions but she knew that, at that time, she would not have been able to do a good job in the timeframe the contract needed to be done. To accept the work would have threatened the values that formed the very fabric of Arrow Messenger Service's culture: the extraordinary attention to service and client satisfaction.

This difficult decision ultimately proved the right one.

When you turn business down for the right reason and in the right way, very often it will come back to you.

A few years after turning down the $500,000 contract, Apelbaum got to bid on another large contract. Neiman Marcus was coming to Chicago and needed a courier company. Apelbaum's anecdote proved to be a great selling point. She convinced the department store that she understood what it took to service a big account and even offered the company whose business she declined as a reference!

As she reflects back on her thirty-year plus entrepreneurial journey, she recounts:

My desire was to earn a decent living to support my son and to be the master of my own fate. I wasn't looking for power. I was looking to earn a living. And I was looking to never worry about working for someone whose ethical behavior was different than mine.

Looking to the future, Apelbaum described the goals she has for her company and the concern she feels about its continuity:

We have reinvented ourselves. There continues to be massive change in the world of delivery; therefore, to ensure continuity, we are moving forward with our facility division, working to build the same reputation that we have enjoyed for over thirty years in our messenger division. I'm trying to figure out what my exit strategy is going to be. I am grooming the executive team (Mark Apelbaum, Tom Krier, and Brenda Brown) to be responsible for the day-to-day operations of this business that is open 7 days a week, 24 hours a day, 365 days a year. I'm also trying to live in a healthier body, that's a goal. But for now, I'm happy I got to get away for three months and to see that Arrow Messenger Service is in good hands if I'm here or not. Life is good.

REFERENCES

Alvarez, S.A., and G.D. Meyer. 1998. Why do women become entrepreneurs? In *Frontiers of entrepreneurship research*. Wellesley, MA: Babson College.

Boden, R. 1996. Gender and self-employment selection. An empirical assessment. *Journal of Socio-Economics* 25 (6): 671–82.

Buttner, E.H. 2001. Examining female entrepreneurs' management style: An application of a relational frame. *Journal of Business Ethics* 29 (3): 253–69.

Center for Women's Business Research. 2007. *Top facts about women-owned businesses.* Washington, DC: Center for Women's Business Research. http://www.cfwbr.org/facts/index.php.

Gundry, L.K., and M. Ben-Yoseph. 2003. Women entrepreneurs in the new millennium: Recent progress and future directions for research, entrepreneurship development, and teaching. In *Entrepreneurship: The way ahead,* ed. H. Welsch. New York, NY: Routledge.

Paine, L.S. 1994. Managing for organizational integrity. *Harvard Business Review,* March/April: 106–17.

Robinson, S. 2001. An examination of entrepreneurial motives and their influence on the way rural women small business owners manage their employees. *Journal of Developmental Entrepreneurship* 6 (2): 151–67.

Vyakarnam, S., A. Bailey, A. Myers, and D. Burnett. 1997. Towards an understanding of ethical behavior in small firms. *Journal of Business Ethics* 16 (15): 1625–36.

Chapter 2

Integrating Personal, Professional, and Corporate Values as an Empowering Leadership Model: Anne L. Arvia

The ideal organization is one that empowers its people. If you do that you can do anything.

One of the leadership challenges in today's changing business environment is how to integrate one's personal values in a competitive arena where ethical issues seem to be part of everyday business. An important factor affecting managerial moral judgment is how managers and professionals prioritize personal, client, corporate, and professional responsibilities. The dilemma of which should take precedence is well illustrated in the number of corporate scandals we have witnessed in the past five years. Moreover, in every institutional setting there are some practices that do not encourage independent decision-making nor provide avenues for questioning what might be, by standards outside the organization, unacceptable activities. Sometimes, too, professionals as well as managers become so involved in their roles and what is expected of them by their clients or company that their judgments become identified with what they perceive to be their role responsibilities (Werhane 1999).

We are enmeshed in a collection of overlapping social, professional, cultural, and religious roles each of which makes moral demands. This becomes problematic when the demands of a particular role become confused, when these demands come into conflict with another role, or when role demands clash with societal norms or common sense morality. For example, the lawyer who protects a known repeated murderer, the psychologist or priest who honors the confidentiality of a criminal's confession, or the reporter who witnesses a spouse committing a crime face role conflicts because of contradictory demands of the profession, religious vows, personal ties, and

Anne L. Arvia

commonly held societal moral norms. Sometimes in business, the pressure to be competitive, efficient, and profitable can conflict with demands of common morality not to lie, steal, or cheat, or with professional demands of transparency and public accountability. Andy Fastow, the former CFO (Chief Financial Officer) of Enron, coached Little League and was called a "mensch" by his rabbi. He would never think of stealing from either organization, but at Enron he was able to bracket these moral convictions so that his behavior as CFO was different.

Role morality can constrain ordinary moral reactions. Sherron Watkins, a former manager at Enron, became an inside whistle blower. Observing what she believed to be unethical and illegal activities when Enron booked losses to off-book partnerships, she wrote an anonymous letter to Kenneth Lay, then CEO (Chief Executive Officer) of Enron, stating her doubts about these activities. She saw herself as a manager with the important role of flagging improprieties. But Watkins did not blow the whistle outside Enron, despite her accumulation of good data to support her suspicions. She was herself first in the role as Enron manager, placing company loyalty rather than professional, public, or shareholder interests first (Swartz and Watkins 2003).

In contrast, at WorldCom, the vice president of internal audit, Cynthia Cooper, began to question outside auditor Andersen's method of financial audits. Following the mandate of WorldCom's CFO, Scott Sullivan, billions of dollars in operating expenses were being booked as capital expenses, thus allowing WorldCom to show a profit instead of a loss for 2001. Both Sullivan and the Andersen auditors violated their professional code as auditors in countenancing these practices. Andersen may have placed the demands of its client, WorldCom, as more important than its independent professional obligations. Only Cynthia Cooper and her team of internal auditors, who redid the Andersen audit and eventually went to the Board of WorldCom with her findings of fraud, prioritized their personal values of honesty and truth telling and the mandates of the professional auditor (AICPA) code before their loyalty to WorldCom (Mead, Wicks, and Werhane 2005).

What can be learned from these episodes is that scenarios such as accounting fraud tend to repeat themselves when one lacks a perspective on one's role, one's institution and its demands, and when one fails to integrate one's personal, social, and professional values into business practice. Unless a manager can disengage herself from the context of a specific problem and challenge herself to evaluate that problem from her personal and professional values perspective, decisions remain parochially imbedded such as to result in an iteration of the very kinds of activities that invite repeated moral failure. An integrative approach to values-based corporate leadership linking personal, professional, and managerial principles can help executives to think more carefully about the issues they face in business (Freeman et al. 2006). Anne Arvia exemplifies this sort of leadership.

Anne Arvia had planned a long career as CFO at ShoreBank, the largest entity in ShoreBank Corporation (a twenty-affiliate company with approximately $2 billion in assets). But when ShoreBank's President, Margaret Cheap, unexpectedly developed a fatal cancer and passed away, Arvia, to her own surprise, was selected as the new bank president. Suddenly she was catapulted into a leadership position with an inherently steep learning curve.

SHOREBANK: A LEADER AMONG COMMUNITY DEVELOPMENT BANKS

Founded in 1973 through the acquisition of The South Shore Bank, ShoreBank became the first community development financial institution in the country. The bank was located in what was once one of the poorest neighborhoods in Chicago, the South Shore. It established a reputation for innovation in community development work, primarily focusing on underserved neighborhoods.

> *As the last bank in the South Shore neighborhood, the government denied The South Shore Bank's petition to leave the neighborhood. ShoreBank took it over with the notion that every community has to have access to a checking account, a savings account, and the availability of credit, otherwise how do people in these communities buy a home? They don't. How do the entrepreneurs start their business? They don't.*

In the early days, ShoreBank attracted depositors by visiting customers in their homes and talking with neighbors about the basic services such as establishing a checking or savings account. They slowly proved that a strong, independent banking presence in the neighborhood could help a community get back on its feet. One of the early initiatives was to provide credit to people who did not have adequate collateral or a good credit rating, the sort of person that banks at that time habitually turned down for loans.

Some banks approached providing credit with the attitude of, "We're helping you and you should be happy to take this money." But what worked in our organization was partnering with the entrepreneurs in the community and giving them a chance to do what they do best. They are the ones who really understand what they need to make their business work and they use that business to help the community as a whole.

It soon became well known that ShoreBank listened to what people wanted and lent money on good will to entrepreneurs who had a record of honesty and integrity, rather than collateral. This "lending on trust" in turn created a reputation which they have been building on ever since. The bank focused its lending on people who would rehab apartment buildings and houses in the neighborhood, and today the South Shore neighborhood is a safe, middle-class community. Thirty years later, ShoreBank has successfully lent over $1 billion to more than 40,000 businesses and individuals in its largest communities and has been profitable every year since 1975. It has also expanded in several states and even has operations in developing nations such as Kenya, Pakistan, and Bangladesh.

From the beginning, ShoreBank had the distinctive mission of working with customers by empowering them to build and improve their own community. By customizing the traditional bank products, the bank not only made a profit but also created a competitive advantage for the organization.

The bank started by really listening to what customers wanted, because we couldn't bring the standard bank product in. It wasn't going to work. Market values didn't mean anything there, and so to make a loan in your traditional real estate market value way made no sense. The borrowers needed really flexible cash. They needed higher loan-to-value ratios. And they needed somebody to help them think about how to manage a property. We had to create what was going to work there, which then created a niche competitively for ShoreBank that was highly successful.

THE BUILDING BLOCKS OF A SUCCESSFUL PRESIDENT AND CEO

Arvia graduated from Michigan State University with a bachelor's degree in accounting. She joined Crowe, Chizek & Company as an Accounting Manager in 1985. Even though she had offers from top tier accounting firms, she chose to join a smaller firm where she felt she would be given a broader scope of responsibility. She was correct, as Crowe, Chizek was on the brink of massive expansion. She took a job based in South Bend, knowing that the company was soon planning to expand to Chicago. Within a year, Chicago beckoned for Arvia and she moved with the company.

In 1991 Arvia left Crowe, Chizek for ShoreBank and held a number of positions there, all of which gave her increased leadership responsibility. She started out as Assistant Controller, then Vice President and Controller in 1993, rising to Senior Vice President three years later before being named CFO in 1998. When Arvia became CEO, she was President Margaret Cheap's right-hand person, so she saw firsthand how the bank was run. At that time, Arvia didn't anticipate the title of President. She had never been a lender and assumed that most bank presidents had to have lending experience.

When she ultimately took over as President, Arvia became an anomaly in the industry. Her age and gender distinction presented numerous challenges.

A lot of women talk about the glass ceiling, and the world of banking is definitely a man-dominated world—only 5% of bank presidents are women, and when you add my age on top of it only 7% of bank presidents are under 40. But I always think of it as a challenge to overcome, as opposed to an obstacle.

I attended an event for a prominent professional, male-dominated organization downtown at the Chicago Club and when I walked in the woman behind the desk said, "You know you're late? You were supposed to be here an hour ago!" and I thought to myself, Late? I'm early! The meeting hadn't even started. I pointed to my name tag on the desk and said, "Well, that's my name." She said, "Oh my gosh, I thought you were part of the catering staff!" We women don't help each other a lot! And there have been countless of those occurrences throughout my years in public accounting. I've talked with a lot of women about this and some feel that they have been held down by it and haven't gotten certain opportunities because of it. These are obstacles and one can see them as such, but I've always kind of relished when it happened. I sit quietly and wait for my opportunity to let my work shine. In a way that's harder and it doesn't give you that immediate leg up when you walk in the room. Some people see that as a disadvantage. I've just thought of it as one of the challenges in making sure that my work, my credibility, and my ability are going to be what succeeds.

IMPORTANT MENTORS AND THE QUEST FOR WORK/LIFE BALANCE

Arvia cites two professional mentors who helped support her in significant ways along her career path. They influenced her work style and demonstrated how to support employees through respect and encouragement.

I had a Partner at Crowe, Chizek named Frank Arford. He treated people with the utmost respect at all levels. He was also thoughtful, very committed, very passionate about his work, and consistent in his delivery and methods. When he said he would do something, he would do it. I still have contact with him. He's just somebody that I have always gone back to, asking how would he handle things in my situation.

And then Margaret Cheap, the former CEO. I only worked with her for a short time, but we were very, very close. She had a lot of the same characteristics as Frank, but she also was extremely visionary and strategic, and playful too. She was that person who just lit up the whole room. You just knew that Margaret had arrived. She wasn't the center of attention. She just had a tremendous presence about her that made people be drawn to her, in a very down-to-earth way. I learned a lot about business from both of them.

I think growing up in a man's world and finding a woman mentor was important—even though Margaret never had children and didn't have the work/life balance issues that I've dealt with, she was an important mentor. I was told partway through my career that I needed a woman mentor who had dealt with some of the work/life balance issues. I always had more men mentors and people who worked more than they played. Margaret worked more than she played, but she had a zest for life that was contagious.

Arvia is still looking for a modern-day mentor to bounce ideas off of and, like other women at the top of their profession, sees the loneliness of the position as one of the few downsides to the job. Although she loves people and interacts fully with her staff, she cannot always discuss matters which are the pressing issues of the day and has to keep a lot "inside." She does, however, try to pass the torch by mentoring others. She says she has "coaching relationships" with most of her staff.

When Arvia took the reigns of ShoreBank, she relished the challenge and thrived with the opportunity she had been given. But, even the best career is rarely without stress. With a husband and two children, it is a constant balancing act, which, she admits, she never quite wins. Fortunately, her husband, a former CPA, stays at home and runs domestic affairs. Arvia admits she is lucky to have a partner who is comfortable with being a househusband. Her values of family and balance are embedded in her management style, as she endeavors to treat people the way she would want to be treated.

BUILDING CHANNELS OF OPEN COMMUNICATION AT SHOREBANK

When Arvia joined ShoreBank in 1991, one of her first priorities was to help improve the management culture in the organization. She supported massive change in the bonus structure by introducing performance reviews and a performance management system. Her team quickly felt empowered and included. This change helped to permeate a culture of communication and trust throughout the business.

When asked how others within the organization might view her leadership style, Arvia explained the importance of getting to know her employees. She strives to create an atmosphere where open communication is an integral part of the company culture.

I try to be very open and down-to-earth. I work very hard to know all 400 employees by name and a little bit about each one. I spend a lot of energy doing that. From a business standpoint they know day-to-day what's going on. They know better than I do, in a lot of ways. I want them to feel comfortable enough—Teller, Senior Manager, whatever—to pick up the phone and to call me. And it does happen. The person who delivers my mail walked in the other day and talked to me about a branch closing that had happened and the customer's perspective. It's wonderful that he felt comfortable enough to do that. I hope that that translates into mutual respect and that they know I value their opinion.

I think that's the most important thing that I can do—consistent, fair, respectful treatment of everybody, whatever your title is. I always tell people that if a Teller calls me, and the Chairman calls, I'd call the Teller back first. If a Teller is calling me, something's really wrong and it's likely to be systemic.

Arvia was clearly well respected by her staff at ShoreBank and, being part of a community-based business, her people skills were invaluable. She is convinced that the relationships she has built with her employees helped enhance the strong communication channels within ShoreBank. She never set barriers and admits to being a perfectionist. She respects and values everyone on her team and tries to be fair and consistent in her treatment of her staff, even though she describes herself as being tough.

CHANGE MANAGEMENT AND BUILDING THE SHOREBANK ADVANTAGE

In her classic *Harvard Business Review* article, "Ways Women Lead," Judy Rosener suggests that two of the distinctive and characteristic features of women in leadership positions are their ability to engage in interactive leadership relationships with their managers and employees and a preoccupation with empowering others. Rosener does not mean to imply that men do not do this, but suggests that empowerment is almost a mantra for women in leadership positions (Rosener 1990).

In 2001 Arvia embarked on a massive change initiative within ShoreBank called "Building the ShoreBank Advantage" (BSA). Management succession was a key issue to be addressed during her tenure, since all four founders of ShoreBank were no longer involved in the day-to-day management of the bank. She also wanted to create a whole new environment within the bank and to change the culture from one that was product/silo-driven to one with a focus on customer service.

The new environment was more customer-centric, as opposed to the traditional product focus. Arvia explains this distinction and why this change was important for ShoreBank:

Most banks are organized around products, so you have product specialists in mortgage lending and commercial lending, and they become product specialists. But in doing this, they silo their customer relationships. It's a much better customer for the organization if we have deposits and other services. We needed to change the culture of the organization from one of less consistency to one where accountability was an organizational value. We needed to rally the troops around the bank's mission.

Arvia created a working group known as the IOC (Implementation Oversight Committee)—a cabinet of four people who developed an initiative that implemented a massive culture shift for ShoreBank. The IOC created nine teams including people from across all levels and departments, and gave them a recommendation that had been made by outside consultants. Each team was charged with creating ownership around that recommendation. There was much discussion and changing of the recommendation until every team was satisfied with the final outcome. It was a very exciting and eye-opening exercise completed by diverse teams. For example, a commercial lender may have found himself on the retail deposit team so that he could bring a different point of view to that division.

A massive process was created with specific deadlines and timelines, objectives and goals and, consequently, the "Change Monster" was born.

He became our mascot and symbol of change. We know people are really afraid of change naturally, but it also creates a lot of opportunities, so we rewarded people with these little green toy monsters. People from across the organization would call me and ask how they could get their Change Monster. I would say, "Well, if you've demonstrated behavior that's in support of the change, I'll send you one." It became such that you had to have a Change Monster.

What was really great about this whole process was that the nine teams did their work and we thought that they would be done with the initiative in a year. But they all came back and said they wanted to collaborate more across the organization; that's what they thought made sense. They said, "We want to organize around these customer segments that we know we're really good at. Let's get rid of some of these things that we aren't doing so well. But none of it will work unless we raise the quality of service across the bank. And by that we mean both how we treat each other internally, and how we treat the customer." One hundred percent of the teams came back and said the same thing. So we responded by creating BSA Phase II to address those specific issues. This took another year and some great implementation and execution plans came out of all that.

We were very public about benchmarking the successes as we moved forward. Now the whole bank, from the janitor on up, is tied to the same goals. We have a three-tiered plan where there are bank-wide goals, department goals, and individual goals that all line up around our triple bottom line performance of profit, community development and conservation, quality, and then employee satisfaction. Everyone knows that if they have an individual goal, for example Teller differences, that goal relates somehow to the overall bank-wide goals. They can see that connection. It makes them feel more a part of the team. There's been a massive shift in the collaboration, expectations, and the way we've done the whole conversion of our reporting systems, of our management systems, and our accountability systems across the board. And during that whole time we were posting record profits and record development.

The project was also a lot of fun and included one-on-one meetings and "Lunches with the President" where Arvia met every single one of her staff so people could talk openly with her. With the new plan, everyone was committed to the same goal of wanting to be the best bank and an innovative leader in the community development world.

ACHIEVING FINANCIAL SUCCESS BY EMPOWERING EMPLOYEES

For Arvia, working in a community development institution was her first dream job. Arvia is constantly driving herself and continues to strive for the best. ShoreBank married the two things that she loves in a very impactful way—the business and the social values of helping communities. When asked how she integrates her personal values at work, Arvia says:

I come back to respect and inclusion. It's who I've always been. The old adage, treat people the way you want to be treated, is very much how I try to live my life. That drives everything I do. Of course I want to be successful and I'm a perfectionist. The values of family and people in general are really important to me and so I push those, sometimes to a fault. If you look at my calendar, nobody gets a "No." I find room to put them on my calendar. It doesn't matter what their topic is. I just don't set barriers. I never want to say no.

Arvia's leadership style is effective not only in empowering employees through respect and inclusion, but also in achieving unprecedented financial results. Under her direction ShoreBank achieved an efficiency ratio of 54%, compared to their competitors who are at 58% (where the lower the number the better). This number is especially astounding when you consider they used to be at a 65% efficiency ratio.

No one believed that we could ever get even close to our peer's efficiency ratio, let alone be beating them consistently. We said, "Why not? We have to be able to do this!" As a community development bank, we should be able to run the business side of it better than anybody so we can have the extra resources to do the innovations we need on the community development side. We know it costs us money to be creative and to be out in a community where nobody else wants to play.

Arvia is quick to credit her staff for the bank's outstanding financial achievements. When the bank achieved her goal of doubling ShoreBank's assets within five years—a goal that was achieved in 2007 with $2 billion in assets—she credited the power of her staff's communication skills in coming up with a vision to achieve that goal. A further initiative has been to set up an international fund to invest in underdeveloped countries' financial institution structures. When she left the bank in 2006, this initiative was still in progress.

At ShoreBank, Arvia says that the people were her greatest strength. She always endeavors to hire people smarter than herself and enjoys working with people who are constantly challenging and pushing her. Her mantra is that if you can empower people, you can achieve anything.

The ideal organization is one that empowers its people. If you do that you can do anything. With any strategy, if you have people who feel empowered and are capable, that's the driver.

THE EXPLORATION: DISCOVERING THE RIGHT NEXT STEP

Arvia's decision to leave ShoreBank came after a full year of intense self-examination. Throughout 2005 she worked closely with an executive coach to determine the career aspects that would best fulfill her professional and personal needs.

You have to be thoughtful about what you want before you make a major career change. A lot of people make a change because they are running away from things and I wanted to be sure I wasn't doing that. You have to be sure that developmentally you are getting as much out of the company as you are putting in, and although I really respect the organization, in many ways I had outgrown ShoreBank.

As a result of this process, Arvia came up with five nonnegotiable desires for her next position:

- A complex industry
- A business that is growing or transforming
- A large company
- A company led by a visionary leader
- A culture with high values

Partway through this process Arvia realized that she could not fulfill those desires in any position within ShoreBank. But, to ensure that she completed this self-assessment and career shift in a deliberate and meaningful way, Arvia refused to entertain any job offers during the yearlong process.

She hired a researcher to seek out companies that fit her criteria and leveraged the experiences of her executive colleagues, especially those who had successfully shifted industries. She met with top Chicago CEOs at companies such as BlueCross BlueShield, Exelon, and Sara Lee, to understand how they had achieved success.

When Arvia finally emerged from this exploration and started to look for new opportunities, she had a serendipitous meeting with a top executive recruiter. Arvia was intrigued by an opportunity the recruiter suggested at Nationwide, one of the largest insurance and financial services industries in the world. Although Columbus, OH was not even on her radar as a city to consider for her next step, she decided that she would give it a chance and prove to herself that she could get the job. *When I walked away from the interview process I knew that this was where I wanted to work. The industry is complex and growing and the company's core values really mesh with my own.*

Today Arvia is the President and CEO of Nationwide Bank, founded in 2006. In this role she has the opportunity to set the direction for the bank and to set the course for how the bank will be run.

I am really excited about the future of Nationwide Bank. I made a very deliberate choice when I took this job and I feel confident that it was the right decision for me professionally and personally. From a leadership standpoint, I work hard to empower my employees, but ultimately the organization has to have the right foundation to reach its full potential. You can offer the right financial products. You can create an effective customer service process. But if the organization isn't built on strong values or if the culture doesn't empower employees to put the customer first, you won't achieve your financial goals.

REFERENCES

Freeman, R.E., K. Martin, B. Parmar, P. Werhane, and M. Cording. 2006. Leading through values and ethical principles. In *Inspired leaders,* ed. R. Burke and C. Cooper, 149–74. London: Routledge Taylor and Francis Group.

Mead, E., A. Wicks, and P.H. Werhane. 2005. *Cynthia Cooper at WorldCom.* Charlottesville, VA: Darden Publishing, UVA E 279.

Rosener, Judy B. 1990. Ways women lead. *Harvard Business Review,* November–December: 3–10.

Swartz, Mimi, and Sherron Watkins. 2003. *Power failure.* New York: Doubleday.

Werhane, Patricia H. 1999. *Moral imagination and management decision-making.* New York: Oxford University Press.

Chapter 3

Situational, Transforming Leadership in a Male-Dominated Organization: Margaret Blackshere

Our deepest concern is for working families. We can work with everyone that wants to work for working families.

Margaret Blackshere, first woman president of the Illinois AFL-CIO (American Federation of Labor and Congress of Industrial Organizations), a labor federation with about 1.2 million members, is an example of a situational leader, someone who can step into various leadership roles, adapt to a new situation, and repeatedly be a successful and powerful leader (Northouse 2004, 91). As a situational leader, the origins of Blackshere's flexibility developed in early childhood.

My mother served in Vietnam during the War, and she raised my sister and me by herself after I was 3. In an all-female household, there were never chores that were "boy chores" and "girl chores." There wasn't anything I couldn't do. Rewiring a lamp, laundry, whatever it was, my mom did it so I thought I could. I never had a belief in limitations. If you have goals and you're not hurting other people then you can achieve them.

Her mother made sure her daughters were well prepared for the future and they quickly learned every skill from rewiring to laundry, and covered all the household chores. This taught Blackshere that there were no limits; if her mother did it, Blackshere believed she could do the same, and she learned to set high goals for herself from an early age.

Blackshere came from a deeply religious background and began early adulthood studying to be a nun. This experience gave her a strong urge to "give back" to her community. Although she has had a lifetime commitment

Margaret Blackshere

to her religious convictions, Blackshere found that being a nun was too restrictive, so she left to attend college at Southern Illinois University (SIU) in Edwardsville.

RISE IN THE LABOR RANKS

Blackshere began her career as an elementary school teacher, but early on she became involved in the politics of education. As she describes this,

> *I went to school to become a teacher in the sixties and we thought we could do anything, improve things, and make life better. I was making $3,000 a year. The district built a new school and they didn't consult the teachers. Teachers didn't get treated with respect. I looked around in my community in Southern Illinois and there were steelworkers and mineworkers, who belonged to industrial unions. These folks were really doing well because they belonged to a union and worked together. Given this successful model, at the school district where I taught we formed a union and went to our superintendent, arguing that we deserved some respect and to be paid adequately. He seemed to agree. Then later he said he couldn't do it. We were outraged that he had lied to us and never had any intention of improving our working conditions. I couldn't understand if you were doing something good why people disagreed with you. But this was a good lesson for me— I realized that not everyone agreed with you, even when the cause was worthwhile....*

Undaunted, she helped organize a five-week school strike against the super-intendent. She begged others not to cross the picket lines, and as she describes this, *We got very militant*. Because as public employees their strike was illegal, she and some of her colleague-organizers were jailed. However, there were only two cells at the local jail, so they were sent home at night to sleep. But every day Blackshere showed up at the jail, always accompanied by her two children, ages 3 and 5. As a result, she was elected president of her local teachers' union in Madison, IL.

Her political instincts were further encouraged when she went back to school for a master's degree in Urban Education at SIU. Having taught only in urban settings and primarily to economically challenged children, she decided that she needed to become more sensitized as to what was important to children living in poverty. Although she was studying urban education, her political life developed during this period. There was a refer-endum for new land for the university, and she joined the student council working to pass the referendum. As she described it, *we (students) would take potential political contributors and supporters up in helicopters to survey the property. The owner shot at us. [Again] we were doing a good thing and some people didn't agree. . . .*

The following year she helped to form Teachers in Politics, having determined that the only way to make changes is through participating in the political system. Although none of the Teachers in Politics candidates won their elections, the experience was life-changing for Blackshere. She began to realize that participation is only one part of politics; the second is to network and communicate with as many constituents as possible. So Blackshere began working for other local people on their election campaigns. Later, she was elected to the vice presidency of the Illinois Federation of Teachers and Chair of the Legislative Committee of the Union.

Because of her political experience and knowledge and in order to support her children, Blackshere reluctantly gave up teaching, which she loved, and became a lobbyist for the Illinois Federation of Teachers. She was dedicated to improving the salaries and working conditions of teachers, but she also immediately began networking with other lobbyists, working with other unions, and devoting time for causes both related and unrelated to education. Thus, Blackshere began to expand her model of "giving back" and committing herself to her newly found conviction that networking creates more alliances than conflicts, by working on what she believed were important pieces of legislation for the community. She also developed coalitions with manufacturing associations, chambers of commerce, and other business groups. Her idea was that if companies make profits, teachers and workers would benefit as well.

In 1993 when a vacancy came up for a Secretary/Treasurer at Illinois AFL-CIO, always willing to adapt to a new situation, Blackshere was asked to serve because she knew so many people outside of her union and could be relied upon to garner votes. Today she is often labeled as "the first woman labor lobbyist," "the first woman Secretary/Treasurer," and "the first woman President of a state federation." First and foremost though, she labels herself a trade unionist.

The AFL-CIO is a voluntary federation of fifty-four national and international labor unions. The AFL-CIO includes more than 10 million workers working in virtually every part of the economy. Its mission is to bring social and economic justice by enabling working people to have a voice on the job, in government, in a changing global economy, and in their communities (AFL-CIO 2007).

AN UNPRECEDENTED CONTEST

There is a long-standing tradition within the Illinois AFL-CIO that the incumbent Secretary/Treasurer automatically becomes President without any opposition when that position becomes vacant. Blackshere assumed that that tradition would continue. However, for the first time in union history, Blackshere's candidacy to President was contested. One flyer questioning her election contended that the federation did not need a kindergarten teacher, but during the election a worker spoke up in her defense, arguing that he had adored his kindergarten teacher! In the end, in 2000 Blackshere was elected and became the first woman to head the Illinois AFL-CIO.

Accepting the Presidency Blackshere said,

I felt that I had a role to play. The Labor Movement traditionally does a wonderful job on legislation, collective bargaining and politics. I thought we should do more—coalition building, community effort...so that was my campaign....If we want to grow this labor movement then we would need to expand what we do, we can't just take care of our current members, and we need to take care of working people.

Blackshere inherited an office with a professional staff of twenty-five, none of whom was a person of color. The Executive Board was all male. The federation had no well baby care insurance coverage and no mammogram coverage, neither of which had been necessary for the all-male Board nor for officers, most of whom were beyond childbearing age. This situation, which she found intolerable, led her to redefine and expand her role as a union leader. Before long, Blackshere had these benefits in place and became well known for being a pioneer in that regard.

TRANSFORMING THE CULTURE

She then began working to transform the culture at the Illinois AFL-CIO, a traditionally all-male organization. The Board of the federation now has seven African-Americans, two Latinos, and eight women. Her goal is *to grow the labor movement and make it comfortable with all working people, immigrants, women, gays. This is a struggle because we have a lot of folks who think they're* *doing fine even if their organization is not. [We have] high priced labor leaders, making $300,000 a year; I make $125,000.* With a diverse board she does not feel alone when she presents an idea to the board. Still, her advice is never to presume, and never to present an idea without being able to back it up with good, solid information. A recent example is that of a fellow President of another union who nominated his Secretary/Treasurer for a further term without asking whether his associate would like to continue. The Secretary/Treasurer stood up at the convention and refused the nomination.

Blackshere's leadership style as President of the Illinois AFL-CIO might be best described as "transforming." One of the important elements of effective leadership is exemplified in the relationships that develop between a leader and her colleagues, managers, and employees. Motivating managers and employees, particularly in an organizational context where trust, creativity, good decision-making, and efficiency are at stake, can make an enormous difference in the firm's long-term effectiveness in highly competitive markets, whether those are financial markets, commercial markets, or labor. Engendering trust and loyalty among one's constituents and retaining the best managers and employees are critical for adding value. Moreover, a transforming leader is a person who not only develops strong relationships with her followers or employees. Transforming leadership describes "a relationship of mutual stimulation and elevation that converts followers into leaders and may convert leaders into moral agents. [This] occurs when one or more persons *engage* with others in such a way that leaders and followers raise one another to higher levels of motivation and morality" (Burns 1982, 5). Thus, a transforming leader engages with, and brings along, her followers and at the same time her followers affect how one leads. Together, in this model, followers and leaders work in unison to create or transform the mission, vision, and goals for an organization. The result is not merely mutual respect and constituent "buy in," but a consensus that the process and its outcomes were every participant's responsibility and contribution.

Unlike leaders in hierarchically structured organizations, Blackshere does not view her authority as a matter of power because of her formal authority. Rather, she sees leadership as an ongoing process, and Blackshere sees herself as a team leader, inspiring rather than directing. Her interactions with managers and employees are seldom transactional exchanges of rewards or demotions for superior or inferior performance. Instead, her goal is to coordinate and balance her vision of the union with those of her members and employees, transforming these into shared union goals. This is usually translated into forms of interactive and participatory leadership that empowers members and employees to adopt her vision as their own, while at the same time achieving benefits for workers. Leadership becomes a three-way interaction between union members, union employees, and union officers where each is motivated and sometimes even changed. So the leadership style is more like coaching than directing, more participative than hierarchical.

In this manner Blackshere is trying to transform the Illinois AFL-CIO into an inclusive diverse organization where family and work are equally important. Under her leadership, the Illinois AFL-CIO has lobbied for equal pay legislation which would prohibit employers from paying women less than men who work for the same employer performing equal work. Some of her other priorities have been to push for the passage of living wage legislation for employers that do business with the state and a corporate responsibility bill. Blackshere has made a number of changes for the benefit of women in the workplace. The union now offers paid family medical leave—with this in place, one of her staff who has just had twins can enjoy them for a few months without having to worry about managing on little or no pay. Thanks largely to Blackshere, there are now more women working in the Illinois Governor's office and the U.S. Senator's office and she is very proud to have been able to help with the careers of so many talented people.

THE POWER OF CONSENSUS BUILDING

Blackshere has achieved success not by forcing issues but through developing consensus. One of her secrets is to try to talk the language of her constituents. The world of trade unionism is still largely dominated by men. Fortunately, Blackshere has a passion for baseball and finds that having a genuine, all-around knowledge of the sport has proven to be a real icebreaker when she meets new people and tries to gain their respect. Indeed, when asked about any ethical dilemmas she has faced in her profession, Blackshere relishes telling of a time recently when the Governor of Illinois, Rod Blagojevich, presented her with a baseball bat autographed by the St. Louis Cardinals. For a split second, she agonized about whether she should keep the bat but graciously accepted it. She then reported her gift to her board the following day, as was her procedure, and made sure that her fellow members understood it would not change her relationship with the Governor; but the bat was in her possession to stay!

From an organizational standpoint, Blackshere is committed to improving workplace safety and to improving the wages, hours, and working conditions for workers in Illinois. In her words, she *never stops talking* and describes her job as *bringing people together*. To build consensus she insists on avoiding adversarial relationships whenever possible. To do that she constantly interacts with her members and managers, and encourages all of them to talk to one another. She enjoys delivering messages from the workers to elected officials. She never makes a decision without the prior approval of her board, and she constantly seeks advice and counsel from the membership. At the same time she prides herself on being spontaneous and in coming up with new ideas, so that one cannot always predict what she will think to do next! She is extraordinary at networking and has worked hard to create networking opportunities with other unions and their members. When she has an issue she wants to drive through, Blackshere calls on a lot of others to help place calls and send notes to make sure her voice is heard. In the labor movement, she argues, *when you use this strategy enough times and you've done the legwork, people ultimately listen and things happen.*

THE NEW FACE OF LABOR

One of Blackshere's greatest accomplishments is being able to put a new face on the labor movement. After she won her Presidency and was featured in the media, women would approach her, congratulate and hug her. She was thanked on innumerable occasions by letter and in person as other women recognized that she was an enabler and had broken through a male-dominated world and had the staying power to stick with a difficult situation. She gave other women hope and inspiration. Her mantra is, *take advantage of every opportunity, just do it because it will lead to something and make you a better person.*

Being an ex-teacher has helped Blackshere become a formidable force in the labor movement, and she is transparent about her beliefs and aversions. She tries always to tell the truth even at the expense of hurting someone; she detests liars and slackers. She has a strong belief in family and her faith—Roman Catholic—even though she does not always agree with the Church. She also has a strong belief in herself and trust in others. From an early age, her mother taught her to "keep the ladder below you, never pull it up," a theme that describes her interactions, not merely with her members and employees but with others with whom she is engaged in "giving back" as well. Blackshere tries to help others when she can, volunteering in her community whenever time permits. Blackshere makes a point of sitting on many boards, but refuses to take payment. Instead, if payment is offered, she gives it to charity.

Blackshere's most influential role model was her mother, as she noted earlier. Blackshere cites other role models including Eleanor Roosevelt—always a popular one—and Mary B. Quinn, a woman she met in her early teaching days. Quinn always reminded Blackshere of her own roots and was a real stabilizing force. She taught Blackshere that you have to win in small ways before you can make changes. Quinn also emphasized the importance of family. With this in mind, Blackshere has always taken her children with her in her travels and to conventions. She brags that her sons have grown up into well-balanced men who have attended more conventions than most adults!

Blackshere is mindful that, to keep the union vital, she must keep expanding its work and continue engaging with other unions about future potential coalitions. She cites an example when she recently opened talks with the manufacturer's association with whom the Illinois AFL-CIO has never worked with before. She worked on a strategy to present to her board who will ultimately decide whether the coalition will take place. As this was not a natural partnership for a labor organization, Blackshere had to be convincing and do her research.

Blackshere is very much aware that there is still a degree of corruption in the trade union movement and she is working hard to rid the movement of that. But it takes time. Needless to say, ethics play a large part in this industry and she mentions one occasion when a nonaffiliated union tried to intimidate her when she was in the throes of trying to break them up. Some of their leaders physically surrounded and threatened her. As Blackshere jokes, ethics are easier when you're being intimidated! She has from time to time received anonymous phone calls and threatening letters and her security has had to be improved, but, she is pretty much a fearless person.

Part of sustainable leadership is to create vibrant growth in an organization so that its mission is not lost in trivia and the leadership agenda does not become stale. For the future, Margaret Blackshere worries about factories and mills closing down, often destroying the town's infrastructure. In response to this growing phenomenon, Blackshere wants to grow the labor movement and make it comfortable for all working people. She clearly loves her job and relishes the challenges ahead whether it is working with politicians and minorities or getting rid of trade union corruption. Her devout commitment to workers and to the importance of the labor movement creates a solid values base and positive incentives from which she inspires others. Like most visionary leaders, Blackshere's work is not finished nor will it be in her lifetime. But that, of course, is what inspires her and her constituents to continue with their mission.

On January 17, 2007, Blackshere announced she was stepping down from the presidency of the Illinois AFL-CIO. According to the *Sun-Times*, "She plans to continue her work focusing on global labor issues" (Knowles 2007).

I feel really strongly that we've got to start bringing every worker up, not just our members living in America, but all over the world, otherwise we're all going to suffer. So I intend to work with Third World country people who hopefully want to join a union.

REFERENCES

AFL-CIO. 2007. www.aflcio.org (accessed February 6, 2007).
Burns, James MacGregor. 1982. *Leadership*. New York: HarperCollins.
Knowles, Francine. 2007. AFL-CIO chief to punch out: First woman to hold post names successor. *Chicago Sun-Times* (Chicago) January 17, 55 (final edition).
Northouse, Peter. 2004. *Leadership: Theory and practice*. 3rd ed. Thousand Oaks, CA: Sage Publications.

Chapter 4

The Powerful Influence of Coaching:
Gail Boudreaux

I have brought along some individuals in our talent development program that I think have great promise for the future. So I think my future will be measured by my ability to identify talent that takes us to the next dimension.

COACHING FOR PEAK PERFORMANCE

Effective leaders must develop talent in organizations, and coaching is a necessary tool for ensuring that development occurs (Ting and Scisco 2006). Increasingly, organizations are looking to their "benches," and that can be strengthened through coaching programs that develop internal talent (Hughes, Ginnett, and Curphy 2006). Coaching as a management style has increased in popularity and importance over the last few years, and many organizations, recognizing the role that coaching plays in the achievement of organizational goals, are supportive of coaching cultures. Coaching enables managers to motivate their subordinates to higher levels of performance. This in turn may lead to greater achievement of organizational goals.

Coaching in organizations may be defined as a management style, or as a subset of behaviors that managers perform, that enables people to learn lessons from their experience. Coaching is the "process of equipping people with the tools, knowledge, and opportunities they need to develop them-selves and become more successful" (Peterson and Hicks 1996). The partner-ship of manager and subordinate is committed to improving performance beyond its current levels and emphasizes communication in a relationship that is person-, results-, and action-oriented (Evered and Selman 1989). The one-on-one relationship is key, and leaders also recognize that in addi-tion to enabling and empowering subordinates to contribute more fully, the context in which performance improvement occurs is critical to ensuring

Gail Boudreaux

that individuals, teams, and organizations are able to achieve the results they aspire to.

Gail Boudreaux never used the word "coach" to describe her style of leadership. Yet, it is clear that Boudreaux practices many of the same coaching behaviors that her coaches undoubtedly taught her when she was playing youth sports. *I was very competitive in sports in college and in high school, and my earliest role models were my coaches. I had coaches who actually were not that far away from me in age, who were inspiring and set high goals.*

INFLUENCES FOR SUCCESS

Boudreaux holds the position of Executive Vice President for External Operations for Health Care Service Corporation, a position she acquired after serving as President of BlueCross BlueShield of Illinois. Her motivation in her new position is staying close to the customer and the market, which requires more of an external focus than an internal focus, as well as the responsibility for setting strategies. Boudreaux had the desire to *maintain leadership over our marketing plans and our subsidiaries...and I thought it was more important to help drive the company to results by managing the subsidiaries that deliver those results than the staff functions internally.*

Education was an influential factor in Boudreaux's development as a leader, but not the main one. She attended Dartmouth, which had just recently opened its doors to women, but was still predominantly male at the time. Dartmouth taught Boudreaux to be independent, and she learned how to succeed in a very small and male-dominated environment. And although the educational experiences were influential, Boudreaux *was extremely involved in sports and that had a bigger influence than even the educational components.* Business school in New York, where she was able to structure her own curriculum, gave Boudreaux the skills and background to help build her credentials. *But in terms of leadership style and other things I think they were a component but not the dominant driver.*

Throughout her career, Boudreaux has framed her challenges in terms of opportunities. For example, she has moved frequently and relocated her family, and her willingness to do so has helped her get to where she is today. At one point in her career, Boudreaux lived in one state with her family and commuted to a job four states away; she would leave her home and family on Sunday evenings and return five days later. Boudreaux's biggest challenge is *balancing competing demands from my children.* In addition to her two children, being married to a high-powered executive husband made it difficult for Boudreaux to find enough time to balance full-time commitments to home and career. Her extremely supportive husband helped the family find balance by giving up his career.

Boudreaux also had mentors in her workplaces who enabled her leadership development. Early on in her career, she had male bosses who took an interest in her. Her first boss shared Boudreaux's alma mater, and later on senior executives helped her in development programs. Outside of her formal education, Boudreaux had many opportunities to learn about herself, by engaging in 360-degree feedback programs, formal and informal assessment by peers, coaching, and mentoring. *Throughout my career I've had sort of a history of being assessed, which is helpful and painful. I don't think any of us like it, but you do learn a lot about yourself.* Indeed this assessment early on in her career may have helped the future "leader coach" have a "heightened awareness about the issues that may emerge from the coaching process for and about themselves as leaders" (Ting 2006, 25).

Throughout her career, Boudreaux has worked for very few women and has never had a female boss; mostly male role models helped guide her career. Now Boudreaux strives to be a mentor to her very diverse staff, which although not designed to be, is composed of a majority of women. She is very concerned with taking an active role in the development of all of her staff, because of its importance to her personally. When asked about being a role model and what others would notice in her the most, Boudreaux thinks *it is confidence, and I think it's a willingness to spend time throughout the organization.* Others might also notice her drive, as well as her commitment to her community and family. *I'm overcommitted. And if I need to, I mean I still coach my son's basketball team, I make sure that it's in my schedule, and as I've gotten older I've become much more comfortable with doing that.* Boudreaux's actions demonstrate that she is committed to developing performance within the workplace, her family, and her community.

FROM CAPTAIN OF HER SPORTS TEAMS TO COACH OF HER WORKPLACE TEAMS

Boudreaux captained her basketball and track teams and learned how important it was to her to be able to set direction and influence a team to accomplish results. With her leadership, the corporation has had sustained success and *exceeded all of our targets in the four years I've been here.* The operating success has been accomplished well beyond goals, as the company has been successful financially and as a growth model. According to Boudreaux, a balanced scorecard approach to the company's performance enables them to quantify the operational indicators, such as earnings, growth, and product introductions. Boudreaux shares credit for the success with *the leadership team I've had* and points to the innovation in product and service models as keys to sustaining future success.

Recognizing the importance of human resources, Boudreaux believes that development is also a key factor to the success of the organization. She has begun to create some new areas and departments, and is concerned with the development of individuals to help the organization achieve greater performance levels. In the past, she developed talent and credits the relationships that she still maintains with those individuals as key for helping her past organizations turn things around. As Hughes, Ginnett, and Curphy (2006) note, a relationship based on mutual trust and respect between the leader and the follower is critical to ensuring that the follower will respond favorably to ideas for development. Although her current company, Health Care Service Corporation, was successful before she arrived, she recognizes how critical people development is to continuing and growing the future success of the organization. *I have brought along some individuals in our talent development program that I think have great promise for the future. So I think my future will be measured by my ability to identify talent that takes us to the next dimension.* Boudreaux practices what is termed "coaching for development" as she is concerned about the future of followers and needs to focus that coaching on learning (Hunt and Weintraub 2002).

VALUES INFLUENCE THE LEADERSHIP PROCESS

Boudreaux holds strong personal values formulated from her upbringing and brings those with her into the organizational setting she leads.

I grew up Catholic, and I still am, and I still believe that there's a basis of truth and fairness that is absolutely critical in any relationship and that's how I like others to conduct themselves. We may disagree on a business issue, but we need to be straightforward about what it is....[I]nclusion is also very important.

She is quick to point out that within an organization values play a purpose; *it all comes to a result*. Boudreaux emphasizes the importance of clarity about the organization's objectives, and what it is trying to achieve.

The mission of the mutual company where Boudreaux works is value-laden and strongly aligns with her personal values. One of the reasons that Boudreaux desired the position at Health Care Service Corporation is the strong sense of values that the company holds, including values to deliver to their customers and communities.

> *Our mission is to provide access to and insure healthcare for as many people as we can in the places we work. We can do that first through the products we provide to be far reaching and meet as many needs as we can, including a real focus now on trying to get the uninsured insured, through programs for the working uninsured. The business we are in is healthcare, and . . . at the end of the day, we measure ourselves based on the satisfaction of the services we provide to our customers and our ability, beyond just the business model, to make a difference in the communities that we work in. That's really important, and I think that's what makes this a unique place from the other companies I've worked, which talk about that commitment to their communities, but aren't really that committed to it. It's all about a business value here; this is a business-driven organization.*

Health Care Service Corporation wants to be a *flag bearer* as a non-investor owned health care organization. The company is committed to the communities they do business in and that commitment extends beyond the business benefit to them. They keep employees in the states where they work, build offices, and stay involved in the communities.

> *Broader than the business benefit we're actually having an influence over the healthcare in those states, and actually, nationally, so we serve the customers nationally. How it ties together is really where we spend our money, how we allocate the resources of time, the kinds of products we bring to the marketplace and how we support those products. A service philosophy exists which we call "concierge service," which is you call us, we take you out of the middle and solve your issue for you . . . that goes back to being the employer of choice and the provider of choice for healthcare insurance.*

PERFORMANCE AND THE FUTURE

Performance based on merits is one critical factor in Boudreaux's vision of the ideal organization. *It's values-based, it's meritocracy-based, it's successful. It has a clear vision, and articulated strategy, and people have an opportunity, as far as it's meritocracy based, to succeed. So, your merits are why you succeed, and I think that hits it.* The other critical factor in her ideal organization is that *it's very involved; it's got a broader mission than just making money.*

   Just as coaches are constantly trying to raise the performance level of their players/subordinates, they are also open to their own continuous development as coaches (Evered and Selman 1989). Boudreaux has lofty goals for herself and Health Care Service Corporation as she peers ahead to her future. *My goal is to be the CEO of the company and to continue to be challenged and engaged and make a difference. In that sense, to grow and become a better leader. Those are my personal goals. To be able to take this company to another level too.* There can be little doubt that Boudreaux, the leader/coach, with her focus on performance and development for herself and her followers, will accomplish those goals.

REFERENCES

Evered, R.D., and J.C. Selman. 1989. Coaching and the art of management. *Organizational Dynamics* 18 (2): 16–32.

Hughes, R.L., R.C. Ginnett, and G.J. Curphy. 2006. *Leadership: Enhancing the lessons of experience.* 5th ed. New York: McGraw-Hill/Irwin.

Hunt, J., and J. Weintraub. 2002. *The coaching manager.* Thousand Oaks, CA: Sage Publications.

Peterson, D.B., and M.D. Hicks. 1996. *Leader as coach: Strategies for coaching and developing others.* Minneapolis, MN: Personnel Decisions International.

Ting, S. 2006. Our view of coaching for leadership development. In *The CCL handbook of coaching: A guide for the leader coach,* ed. S. Ting and P. Scisco, 15–33. San Francisco: Jossey-Bass, A Wiley Imprint.

Ting, S., and P. Scisco, eds. 2006. *The CCL handbook of coaching: A guide for the leader coach.* San Francisco: Jossey-Bass, A Wiley Imprint.

Chapter 5

Leading Through Workplace Engagement: Cathy Calhoun

It's hard to keep people engaged in the workplace. The little things count. People spend a lot of their time, energy and talent here, so you've got to find ways of rewarding that.

As President of Weber Shandwick's Chicago office, Cathy Calhoun leads through creating an environment that is aimed well beyond employee job satisfaction to stimulating workplace engagement that spurs outstanding competitive performance. Garnering employee engagement, a relatively hot topic among consulting firms for several years, is now beginning to gain academic interest (Saks 2006). Various studies claim that employee engagement—most simply defined as "a work-related state of mind,... characterized by vigor, dedication and absorption"—is an important yet under-tapped source of competitive advantage (Lockwood 2007). Most of this discussion emanates from a macro human resources perspective concerned with aggregated and measurable consequences of leadership, such as employee recruitment, productivity, and retention. In contrast, Calhoun's example provides ideas for encouraging employee engagement, vividly depicted on a human scale.

Voted by *Chicago* magazine as one of the best places to work in the city, Calhoun's company exemplifies a place where employees go beyond merely getting the job done to investing extra effort for superior client results. Calhoun excels at this feat of business leadership by combining personal drive, frank feedback, and unique rewards, and linking these to her everyday leadership practice.

Calhoun's personal drive comes from a strong work ethic and sense of integrity, and she sets a powerful example for those she works with. Her expectations about her own personal engagement translate into the expectations she has for her staff.

Cathy Calhoun

My job is problem-solving and the buck stops here, so I expect them to be problem-solvers. I always want them to come in with a problem and a potential solution—even if it's not where we ultimately end up, it's important to get in the problem-solving mindset. I want a lot of information, but it needs to be very succinct, boiled down to what I need to know to stay focused and make good decisions. My responsibility as a mother means I can't spend endless hours here. When I'm here, I have to be really productive and my teams know and respect that.

Yet as much as her own sense of engagement with her job is driven by intrinsic motivation and maintaining work/life balance, without hesitation, Calhoun admits that money is a principal motivating factor: *People work for money and should be compensated for that. Women are too afraid to admit that money is one of the main reasons that you work.* Yet for Calhoun, money is not just an end in itself but part of a larger picture in which she sees the financial interdependence between employees and their company.

The ideal organization respects and listens to its employees, appreciates people's life beyond work and makes that possible. But the company also has to be financially sound enough to provide a stable ongoing opportunity for its employees to grow and make money. I think it's a tricky balance— you've got to make money and let your employees have a life.

GREAT EXPECTATIONS

Beyond setting expectations, when needed, Calhoun will give frank feedback to deepen her staff's engagement, pushing them to go beyond limits they might not have realized they had accepted for themselves. For instance, as a public relations firm—the world's largest—Weber Shandwick wants to win the best opportunities to gain media exposure for its clients. Recently, one of the company's clients wanted to celebrate its 200th "Got Milk?" moustache advertisement, the iconic series having run into its 10th year. When one of Calhoun's teams got placement for a print story in *USA Today*, they thought they would come up with a big win. But in Calhoun's words, she encouraged the account manager to give an extra push for a great television placement. Calhoun thought the group had stopped too soon and could do better. Because this was such a huge milestone for the Milk Moustache ads, Calhoun wanted to deliver even more value to the client, one of the agency's most-valued partners. The team did as asked and ended up also getting placement on the highly rated morning talk and news show, *Good Morning America!* Later, the account manager admitted to Calhoun that even though he didn't like hearing it, she had been right to push his team. Reflecting on the experience, Calhoun said

> *I'm not often a cheerleader. It's hard for me to be a mentor in a patient, nurturing way because of the pace and responsibility here. I'm more of a demanding, fast-moving, challenging mentor. My mentors were of that ilk. People say it's tough to work for me, but that they learn a lot. But at the same time, when push comes to shove, my teams know I will always go to the mat for them. Always.*

ENGAGING AND REWARDING EMPLOYEES IN A HIGH-ENERGY WORKPLACE

Calhoun pairs her high standards for performance with unique rewards that encourage employee engagement for the long term. *What counts is to come here every day and feel good about it—that's sustainable.* In part, Calhoun credits Weber Shandwick as a progressive company that doesn't throw up a lot of obstacles. *We are heard and respected. I give the leadership in the company a tremendous amount of credit for that.* (Interestingly, although a significant percentage of its workforce is female, most of the firm's global leadership is still male.) As an industry, PR tends to attract younger, creative, and transient workers. Since their intellectual capital and people skills are the foundation of delivering excellence for clients, Calhoun recognizes that she has to *work really hard so people want to stay and be creative. We've been a "hot shop" in the last few years so we are targeted by our competitors when they're recruiting. We have to always push to provide a unique workplace so we can retain our employees—it's really a business mandate for us. But the best feeling is when people leave to go to a competitor and then "boomerang" back to us. We have nearly* ten "boomerangs" in the fold now which really validates our premise that this is a better place to work with more opportunities.

To do that, Calhoun has created a place to work that keeps her own and her employees' engagement high. She likes that her job challenges multiple facets of her personality.

I'm interested in a lot of different things: my operational hat keeps the business running with my very strong ops team—consulting work, which I love, working with clients—and my new business hat has me going out and selling, making sure the new business keeps coming in. My job allows me to shift gears quickly so I don't get bored. And I get to work with amazing people who have been here for a long time. It's a nice place to be, to do different things, and cultivate a team.

And to keep the workplace interesting and to help her employees deal with the demanding pace and *clients who expect both strategic and executional excellence,* Calhoun has developed initiatives that help everyone be more buoyant. Since her employee population tends to be young (aged 25–35), female, and health-oriented, perks are tailored to their interests. In addition to subsidized health club memberships, free water and fruit are available at work. In-office personal services are also available, including manicures on Mondays and pedicures once a month and periodic chair massages. Such services may seem like luxuries to some, but a fresh coat of nail polish fits right in with the image-conscious world of public relations. On the more practical side, it's a feminine twist on spending time around the old-fashioned water cooler. *It's a terrific time saver for everyone. We even use the time for meeting and catching up. It's hard to keep people engaged in the workplace. The little things count. People spend a lot of their time, energy and talent here, so you've got to find ways of rewarding that.*

On top of such "little things," Calhoun is sure to celebrate successes and encourage creative time away from the office. For example, when the company won a new olive oil account, Calhoun threw a tapas party to show her appreciation. In addition,

A lot of the programs came up through creative problem-solving. People had a need for something that we couldn't quite do. For example, there were a lot of requests for sabbaticals which are hard for us to do, so we came up with a program called "No Boundaries." Ten employees a year are given a chance to experience something they find personally or professionally enriching. Each person receives $1000 and an extra week off. We've had staffers work on a cattle ranch, take a vow of silence at a Buddhist retreat, experience culinary tours in Italy, attend photo excursions in Utah, build houses for Habitat for Humanity. Afterward they write an essay and give a report on the Web site of their experiences to share with the teams. It has turned out to be a great recruiting and retention tool. People need the opportunity and the support to recharge their batteries.

CLIENTS AS PARTNERS

For all her attention to her employees' experience at work, however, Calhoun couches it in terms of value for the client and expects a lot from the client in return.

I love my clients and the work I do. My vision is to be a leader in the workplace, to provide a great place for our workers so we can get a great return on investment for our stakeholders and do a better job than our competitors. The game has really changed for us—we're no longer executionally focused, our clients expect us to be full strategic partners. So we have to nurture our teams to be "thinkers" as well as "doers" and it's not always easy.

At the same time, Calhoun won't give up gains she has made with her employees' engagement just to please a client.

I see myself as a woman of integrity, and I try my hardest to live by simple rules of being honest and straightforward. I'm willing to deliver the bad news instead of waiting for it to catch up to me. I've had to make some tough calls here. For instance, I've walked away from some pretty lucrative opportunities because of the way our teams were treated. You have to say "no" sometimes. And you have to be your teams' advocate.

Calhoun expects clients to *treat us as partners, expect a lot out of us, tell us if we stumble and praise us when we do a good job.* Whether employee or client, Calhoun regards team effort, constructive criticism, and a level playing field as necessary ingredients for doing business with the utmost integrity. In the end, for Calhoun, workplace engagement is a goal to which everyone must contribute.

"Pitching in" is indeed essential to Calhoun's leadership ethic, and she credits her father with teaching her never to turn her nose up at menial things. *I try not to ask them to do anything I wouldn't do—or haven't done before.* While she is technically the boss, she sees herself as working in the trenches. *Although my personality is relatively intense, I also have a fairly casual style: during crunch times, I walk around this place barefoot with my hair clipped up on top of my head.* But Calhoun does appreciate the real benefits of power, which she defines as being *able to take care of the staff and have some flexibility and control for my life and my child's. I have the trust of my superiors and my clients that everything's going to get done, and teams who never disappoint. It's allowed me to put the pieces of my life together in my own way.*

REFERENCES

Lockwood, Nancy R. 2007. Leveraging employee engagement for competitive advantage: HR's strategic role. *HR Magazine* 52 (3): S1(11).

Saks, Alan M. 2006. Antecedents and consequences of employee engagement. *Journal of Managerial Psychology* 21 (7): 600–19.

Chapter 6

Opportunistic Values-Based Team Leadership: Ellen Carnahan

The ideal organization shares a common vision, and each person in the organization takes their role seriously and responsibly. The ideal organization also communicates well and strives to work as a team. In order to hit your common vision you're going to have to work as a team. That's kind of a quid pro quo. You can share a vision and not work as a team and you'll never get there.

According to *Crain's Chicago Business,* the leading journal of Chicago Business, Ellen Carnahan is one of Chicago's most influential women in finance. Until last year, when Carnahan left William Blair Capital Partners (WBCP) to form her own firm, Seyen Capital, Ellen Carnahan was a Managing Director at WBCP where she had led venture capital investments for nineteen years. WBCP managed over $1 billion of capital in seven funds invested in more than 150 high-growth, privately held companies. Headquartered in Chicago, WBCP has an investment bank, William Blair & Company, as one of its partners. This relationship provided high-growth companies with an expanded network of contacts, immediate access to extensive industry research, and particular insight into corporate finance activities and options for selling companies and going public.

FINDING HER PASSION: MAKING UP THE RULES

Carnahan graduated from the University of Notre Dame as an accounting major in the second class of women and holds an MBA from the University of Chicago. She also earned a CPA and started her career at PwC (Pricewater-houseCoopers) in Chicago before moving to Trailer Train Company, the largest operator of railroad flatcars, as Manager of Financial Planning and Analysis. But her interest in software soon led her to join SPSS Inc., an applications software company where she was Vice President of Marketing

Ellen Carnahan

and Planning. Carnahan had very much enjoyed the fast pace, and excitement, of working at a small privately held software company like SPSS. Her bias was that, if you are in a growing business or industry, your career opportunities are much more interesting. Being a risk-taker, she enjoyed the challenges of making things happen to build and create the business. Having cut her teeth as an auditor at PwC, she soon realized that moving fast and making up the rules as you go along in a small, nimble organization was a much better fit for her personality.

At SPSS Carnahan developed the marketing and planning process, helping refuel revenue growth from $8 million to $29 million under her tenure. She was always fascinated with technology and software. It seemed a natural step to join WBCP in the 1980s when technology was the "buzzword." With ten years of management experience in the software and financial services industries and a huge interest in technology, she was an ideal candidate to push forward private equity fund-raising in this growing area.

A NATURAL LEADER WHO RELISHES A CHALLENGE

Carnahan was always ambitious and tells the story of how she got her job at WBCP. She carefully researched all the private equity firms and approached them each by letter. She is the first to admit that, in this electronic age, this approach probably would not work today since the job market has become extremely competitive. With her background of marketing experience in a software company, she got several callbacks because software was just beginning to be recognized as "the next big thing."

Even today, the venture capital and private equity industry is primarily male dominated. In the 1980s it was much more so, and many women had and still have difficulties adjusting to this kind of environment. Carnahan, on the other hand, describes this as a very different experience. As it happened, her university, Notre Dame, had just started admitting women in 1972 and when she entered a year later there were 700 women and 5,000 men in the student body. Notre Dame was breaking with a long-standing male-only university tradition, and this was both challenging and frightening for entering women freshmen.

I always did well in school. I was always a leader in high school—President of the Student Council and that kind of stuff. I naturally stepped up to do those kinds of volunteer jobs. And then when I went to college I decided to try something different. Notre Dame had just started to admit women in 1972 or so when the first full class was admitted and I entered in 1973 in the second full class. And I will tell you, there were only maybe seven hundred women and what was it, five, six thousand men. The discrepancy was huge. It was noticeable. Our dorm had urinals in it that hadn't been taken out. Some of the men didn't want you there because it was breaking with tradition. It was a very different experience. But at the time I had fun. I didn't think it was weird or anything. You noticed it, but you got very comfortable being an outlier, which I think was a very good thing for me to get comfortable with early.

Like some of the older alumni at Notre Dame, many of the men in the venture capital industry initially were not sure about women entering that industry. But given her "training" at Notre Dame, she soon became very comfortable with being an outsider. From that beginning, it has never bothered Carnahan to sit in a room where everyone else was male—she simply got used to it. Carnahan is clearly comfortable "in her own skin." She is exceedingly self-confident of her talents and capabilities and something of an optimist. She does not consider glass ceilings, gender discrimination, or unequal opportunities as obstacles to her career—rather they challenge her to figure out what to do to overcome them.

Her industry, and her position, is not for the fainthearted, though. *If you are investing other people's money, you have to have the courage of your convictions and take great care and fiduciary responsibility. You have to treat other people's money as if it were your own.* To do this job, you need a lot of self-confidence while knowing that not everything will work out positively for every investment. One thing that is helpful, she feels, is putting yourself in the other person's position—trying to think what they would do and look for the common ground. It clearly irritates Carnahan greatly when, on occasion, certain venture capital investments do not work out, but she understands that that is part of the risk of the business.

I can honestly say there's not a day that's gone by that I didn't try to do the absolute best to bring that money that we've invested back, "round-trip."

So even if the company was hopeless and you should walk away or whatever, I always kind of stuck with it and did the absolute best we could for the people that were at that company, for the shareholders and for our investors.

At WBCP Carnahan supervised technology investing and invested approximately 25% of its technology fund across a range of technology companies: semiconductors, communications, and software. Carnahan's specialty is software, and she currently serves as a director of Pavilion Technologies, Vericept, and Compete Inc. Over her long tenure in the private equity business, Carnahan has served on the Boards of more than twenty-five public and private companies.

ROLE MODELS, MENTORS, AND TEACHING TEAM LEADERSHIP

Looking back, Carnahan regards herself as fortunate to have worked for some excellent managers who have pushed and encouraged her. In 1977 at PwC, two of her bosses really helped her and ensured she got promoted early in her career. They taught her the business and gave her responsibility at an early stage in her career. For Carnahan, they were her first role models. Other mentors include her friends, her family, her husband, and her copartner at WBCP, Gregg Newmark, whom she describes as "a great teacher."

At WBCP Carnahan was often left alone to get on with her job—something she relishes. *That work ethic is critical in the fund management business, because you are responsible for coming up with your own workload. A degree of hustle is vital as you have to work up a caseload of companies in which you want to invest.* In this regard, Carnahan doesn't feel that she currently has a mentor but still seeks advice from those around her.

On the other hand, Carnahan works hard at trying to be a mentor, to develop members of her staff, and she is dedicated to team leadership. Team leadership is a very complex process. It begins with making sure the whole team has the same vision, the same mental model of the project, the process, and projected outcomes (Northouse 2004, 208–10). Only with clarity of purpose, careful division of labor, and close collaboration will a team be effective. Carnahan exemplifies that sort of team leadership. At WBCP she met with her team every Monday to talk about potential investments. *This is a time for brutal honesty where one must be careful not to oversell a business but to present a balanced picture and articulate this is a good opportunity. It is a very research-oriented position as you have to have a lot of facts readily available to help support your argument and your success is measured from the actions on the returns you achieve.* She and her team worked in small groups and every member was expected to be equally involved. So communication is absolutely essential. Carnahan also formed teams at different seniority levels to provide an extra layer if some employees did not want to speak with her directly. That way, all issues got raised. When her staff was working on a project to get a fund invested, her whole team was at every meeting and in on every telephone call. Tasks were divided up among the group. A lot of references had to be called so everyone got a flavor of what people were saying. Job assignments were handed out by the Deal Leader (in this case Carnahan) and often the most junior person was actually the one who made sure everyone got their work done—a kind of role reversal came into play. Employees were responsible for their own caseload and so it was difficult to measure people as a group. Still, Carnahan worked hard to monitor her team and to give feedback on a regular basis. Every six months, she talked to each member individually and a meeting was held at the end of every deal to provide a constant flow of information across the team. She is pleased to say that at WBCP she had a good track record regarding her investment judgments.

> To be able to build these businesses, get them financed and work with syndi-cates of people who will all invest together, it's imperative that you are able to work with the group as opposed to always just thinking about yourself.... You have to be able to build trust. You have to have people trust your judgment. A lot of trust is built in our business by just watching somebody over a period of time, so it's really very much an apprentice business. You meet every Monday to talk about the potential investment business and you make a pitch—and very honestly. You don't ever oversell because stuff's going to go wrong. You present a balanced picture and you do your best to articulate why you think this is a good opportunity, and you have to be convincing about that with a lot of facts to support you. [In venture capital business] it is a very research-oriented position that you take. And then, if you see that somebody's not comfortable, then you spend time with them individually to find out why they're not comfortable. You try to get them to communicate with you what their concerns are, and you try to address them. And ultimately, if you cannot, you just drop it and you go on to the next investment. If you can see that your partners are too uncomfortable, you just move on. It's not worth it.

PERSONAL AND PROFESSIONAL VALUES: ONE AND THE SAME

In an industry where companies come knocking on her door to raise funds, Carnahan has to use tremendous integrity and good judgment. Being self-confident and self-determined as well as team-oriented, she was, and still is, more worried about getting to the common goal than her own personal agenda.

Carnahan does not distinguish her personal values from her business values.

> I only have one set of values and I just try to apply them everywhere. [The cor-porate vision] basically says, "to generate superior returns for our investors with integrity and teamwork." I think that's basically what we strive to do. The integrity and teamwork part are pretty key in that....Treat people right—really simple stuff—how would you like to be treated? Greed is a terrible thing. Communicating well is extremely important. I'd rather

over-communicate than anything. You have to really sort out your personal priorities very carefully and you have to hold true to those, because it's easy to let something else creep up and then lose sight of the things that are really important to you. You have to try to stay balanced. It's really hard for me to do. It's easy to be a workaholic and to spend all your time working . . . because you like it.

These values are shared in her hiring and her preoccupation with communicating with her team and her investors, and Carnahan is determined always to treat people with respect. Her vision is basically to generate superior returns for her investors with a combination of hard work and integrity. To this end, Carnahan tries to hire excellent people, because it is her conviction that almost everything is a function of good managers. Seeing how corporate culture can create positive or negative work environments, she looks for people who share the same value system as herself but also encourages people with different viewpoints.

You have to have people who share the same work ethic and sense of integrity and sense of responsibility for handling other people's money—fiduciary obligation, if you will. So, hiring—I think hiring's the best thing. And then training—spending time to train people, mentoring, and communicating. If you have a problem with somebody you have to talk about it. Get it out in the air, clear the air, move on, and focus on the future. Get your bad stuff out and move on.

Carnahan works hard at trying to stay balanced even though she admits to being a workaholic, particularly in trying to do her absolute best every single day to bring the money that has been invested back with added capital. She is proud to say that she feels that she has done well in that regard and has always stuck with her investment decisions, even when she knows she is not going to make the capital gain on an investment. She has learned to do the "hard things" well. Clearly an unpleasant part of her job is when she knows a company is not going to make its milestones and she has to convince everyone to put enough into the company to help wind it down.

Carnahan is not a person to put up with questionable or abusive behavior. Recently serving on a board, she received a number of telephone calls concerning the behavior of the CEO. After gathering all the facts and double-checking her data, she and another board member worked to replace this executive. *It was hard to convince the board that this guy was really doing things that weren't right. It took about a year and I led the effort with another board member. We were right and we hung with it and we brought in some other outside board members that could be more objective to help us see the situation. And they immediately said, "You have a problem here." It took us a year but we replaced the CEO and now the company's doing fine.*

STRIKING OUT ON HER OWN: SEYEN CAPITAL

Discerning a new window of opportunity, last year Carnahan left WBCP to form her own venture capital firm, Seyen Capital, focusing on high growth information technology companies located in less served U.S. markets. According to the Illinois Venture Capital Association Web site, Carnahan was asked why she left WBCP. The dialogue was printed as follows:

> *Question:* "You each previously worked with William Blair Capital Partners (WBCP) and were in the process of raising the firm's eighth private equity fund when you left to start Seyen. What motivated you to leave WBCP to start the new firm?"
>
> *Ellen Carnahan:* "After agreeing to basic terms in July 2005 with William Blair & Company and despite having more than one-third of the target commitments subscribed for a June 2006 closing, we were unable to reach agreement with the firm on final partnership documentation. We therefore suspended fund-raising efforts for Fund VIII in partnership with William Blair & Company. My partners and I were disappointed to leave our long affiliation with William Blair & Company and, prior to this decision, had not planned to form a new firm. Each of us will retain our portfolio responsibilities [with existing WBCP private equity funds] and continue as directors of the companies the prior funds have financed. Along with the other managing directors of the prior funds, we will continue to play a management role in the open funds (WBCP funds V, VI and VII). WBCP funds have raised more than $1 billion in private capital and invested in more than 150 companies since 1982. Of those seven funds, Gregg and I have been active in four and five, respectively" (Illinois Venture Capital Association 2006).

As a cofounder at Seyen, this is a huge opportunity, a huge risk, and one for which Carnahan will be most capable. Despite the stress and workload of forming a new company, Carnahan is keen to focus on the future and to balance work with public service. She sits on a number of corporate boards and on the board of Chicago Communities in Schools. She is the current Chair of The Chicago Network, a Chicago-based organization of women leaders. She is active on several other community boards as well. Carnahan is on the Board of and Co-Chair of the 2007 Annual Entrepreneur Conference of TiEMidwest, the Midwest chapter of the international TiE (The Indus Entrepreneurs) organization. Global TiE is one of the largest, if not the largest, organization fostering entrepreneurship worldwide.

Carnahan was recently selected by the Girl Scouts of Chicago as the 2003 recipient of the Luminary Award as a role model for women and the 2003 Fellowship Award by the Illinois Venture Capital Association. *Crain's Chicago Business* recently ranked her as one of the 100 most influential people in technology.

Opportunistic leadership is often defined as adapting one's skills, style, and opportunities to the best advantage, usually to one's own self-advantage (Northouse 2004, 73). On the contrary, Carnahan is a values-based opportunist. She takes advantage of her skills. She has developed a style that fits well in the highly competitive venture capital industry, and she fearlessly moves to new opportunities, some of which she creates. At the same time, however, she never wavers from her personal values of integrity, trust, and respect for others. At every company where she has worked, she gives her position, her company, her team of employees, and customer-investors her undivided loyal commitment to do the best possible for each of these stakeholders. Her commitment is to be the best in her field without compromising integrity. She is a professional in the sense that doing well for her clients, investors, and work team is of primary concern in whatever corporate setting this takes place.

Carnahan represents a cadre of "new age" managers and executives who give their undivided attention and focus to their work, but who may change the setting of that commitment. Many of these are uncompromising in their integrity and work ethic, but their loyalties are first to their clients and fellow-workers, and only secondarily to the particular company with which they are associated. They often change jobs a multitude of times while advancing their careers with an expertise honed to a particular industry such as the venture capital industry. Such managers often become leaders in their field, but not necessarily CEOs in a company with which they have been associated for a long period of time. This breed of managers and executives are well prepared for the twenty-first century where job security and lifetime employment are no longer viable options, if they ever were. These managers and executives see themselves as well-trained professionals, not as employees and not as permanently committed to one company or firm (Werhane and Radin 2003). Carnahan exemplifies this new breed of managerial professionals who are the exemplars for future managers and executives operating in an ever-expanding and ever-changing global economy.

REFERENCES

Illinois Venture Capital Association. 2006. Interview with Ellen Carnahan, August 16. http://www.illinoisvc.org (accessed February 19, 2007).

Northouse, Peter G. 2004. *Leadership: Theory and practice.* 3rd ed. Thousand Oaks, CA: Sage Publications.

Werhane, Patricia H., and Tara J. Radin. 2003. Employment and employee rights: A retrospective and prospective. *Business Ethics Quarterly* 13: 113–30.

Chapter 7

Challenging the Paradigm: The Positive Role of Negative Mentoring as a Leadership Model: Donni Case

I defined what I thought was good leadership by observing other people who I felt lacked it even though they were in positions of power. That's why I looked to history for people that I thought had faced some extremely dire circumstances. Like Abraham Lincoln and how he managed himself through that. . . .

One of the important elements of effective leadership is exemplified in the relationships that develop between a leader and their colleagues, managers, and employees. Motivating managers and employees, particularly in a corporate context where trust, creativity, good decision-making, and efficiency are at stake can make an enormous difference in the long-term effectiveness of a company in highly competitive markets. Engendering trust and loyalty and, most importantly, retaining the best managers and employees are critical for creating value. Part of that leadership focus is creating a positive "psychological contract" between the leader and their employees, and transparency contributes substantially to that positive climate. In the volatile workplace of the twenty-first century, however, where workforce changes due to mergers, acquisitions, outsourcing, and/or economic exigencies are the norm, creating a positive organizational climate of trust is often difficult. Under the present economic climate, managerial and employee loyalty cannot be counted on. Often, too, in this volatile climate, employee perceptions of what a leader has in mind or what the organization is about can differ significantly from a leader's intentions or the direction of the company. Still, positive management and employee mentoring and support are important both for the employee and for the company, even if job security is no longer an option.

Donni Case

In developing trust, if not absolute loyalty, strong mentor relationships are very important.

> One of the critical types of relationships for career advancement is a *mentor relationship,* in which a senior individual provides task coaching, emotional encouragement, and sponsoring the protégé with top level decision makers.
>
> (Indvik 2004, 280)

Mentoring can make a significant difference in developing leaders, in creating bonds between present and future leaders, and in helping to insure the long-term leadership in a company. Part of being a successful leader is the ability to mentor and to develop other leaders in the organization. Yet, "several studies have documented that women leaders have experienced *lower support* throughout their careers than similarly employed males..." (Morrison, 1992, reported in Indvik 2004, 280). These studies show that in many companies women managers are mentored significantly less either by men *or* by women. It is not surprising, then, that in 2005 where our data ends, there are very few women CEOs in the Fortune 1000 organizations and on corporate boards.

That this is unfair, that it is discriminatory, and that it creates unequal opportunities at the top of organizations should be obvious. But suppose you are a woman manager who finds herself in such an organization? How can one take the absence of mentoring or a negative mentoring relationship and use it to one's own competitive advantage to develop survival techniques and leadership skills? One such example is Donni Case, former President of FRB (Financial Relations Board).

BREAKING GROUND IN THE MALE-DOMINATED WORLD OF INVESTOR RELATIONS

Not many women or men can lay claim to having the same career in the same company for thirty years but Donni Case is an exception to the rule. Clearly someone who is passionate about the field of investor relations, Case relishes the challenges of the industry. As President of FRB, she thrived in what was historically a male-dominated arena and only a personality as feisty and determined as Case could have made it to the very top. Case was one of the founding partners of FRB and National Director of Marketing Intelligence. She also served as the Supervising Partner of West Coast operations as well as the Director of Shareholder Management Services offering proxy, stock surveillance, and corporate governance services.

One of the interesting things about investor relations is that it was a very much undefined business when I started out. Financial Relations Board literally invented the practice of investor relations so we all kind of grew up in it together. I have spent thirty-three years with this company constantly adapting to changing environments. When I started, the [financial services] industry was almost entirely male dominated, and we were marketing our services to the investment community that was also male dominated. I can say the first ten years of my career were exasperating in a lot of respects because as a female, I was discriminated against. Some portfolio managers did not want to meet with me and some clients did not want to meet with me because I was a woman. I found this especially shocking coming from those who had daughters. Again, for perspective, I am talking about the old boys club of 30 years ago.

FRB concentrates on the application of communication, message, and positioning of public companies' corporate or financial brands, and communicating that positioning to the largest portfolio managers in the world. Until April of 2005, Case was responsible for its North American operations. Her business is all about bringing out strategy and message points of companies that differentiate them. Using a combination of research, evaluation, and well thought out predictions of outcomes, those messages are then delivered directly to the investment community. During the last thirty years, Case built relationships with key influencers in the U.S. capital markets by demonstrating to corporate executive clients how and in what ways a portfolio manager views and evaluates that CEO's company's stock.

LEADING WITH A MORAL COMPASS

The oldest of four daughters, Case had a very special relationship with her father.

My father was my big role model. . . .I honestly looked and I tried to find role models that were in business. When I started out there weren't many women, so that was something a little bit against me. I could never relate to the celebrity CEO-types, and there are a lot of other scary characters. I realized very early as a result of my father's incredible ethical behavior that I could never follow those types of people. He was especially impactful on me because I was the oldest of four daughters, and I'm sure if he were alive today he would say that nothing could have been better than having four daughters. I pretty much got to pal around with him, go to work with him and be his sidekick. My father was vice president of manufacturing of a small family-owned company, and he had to deal with family politics, unions, dumping, questionable incentives and other such practices. He never wavered from his moral compass so I knew by his example when the values orientation and behavior of some male colleagues were antithetical to my father's.

From an early age, Case deeply empathized with her father's high ethical standards throughout his employment, and quickly realized that her father never lost his moral compass, even under pressure—an attribute that remains with her today. Case is a woman who does not suffer fools. She ran a fair-minded organization and bad ethical decisions, impropriety, or abuses of any kind were definitely not tolerated. From that standpoint, it is refreshing to find someone at the top of her profession who constantly encouraged her staff to examine issues, offer input, and develop a strong awareness of the risk and reward profile of those decisions. Even though she made the final decisions, she was keen to listen to the voices around her. Like Anne Arvia, and many of the other women leaders we highlight in this study, she worked to empower her staff and was not afraid of confrontation or disagreement.

In regard to the leadership styles of her predecessors,

The people I worked for were brilliant business people, so you have to separate their ability to make and do business and to identify new opportunities in the marketplace from their people skills. I think that many of these leaders early in my career had a "George Patton" approach to leadership. They would stand there and command the troops and tell them exactly what to do. They didn't really want to invite opinion, and they didn't really want to have any kind of a democratic forum. They pretty much thought that they knew it all already, and they even told you precisely how they wanted you to say it. It was a military approach to leadership.

MOVING BEYOND COMMAND-AND-CONTROL LEADERSHIP

How did Case's rise to the top happen in such a male-dominated industry? Case graduated from the University of Illinois, Champaign-Urbana with a BA in Economics. Her first love was classic history, and having written a paper on the economic implications of the Peloponnesian War, she decided that economics had more fascination. At the same time she began to develop her idea of leadership by observing people in history who were in positions of power.

Case remembers the first ten years of her career as being particularly exasperating. It was an era where women were second-class citizens and definitely marginalized.

Men got away with what is unthinkable today. Some really didn't care if they offended their women coworkers, whether it was sexual harassment or inappropriate remarks. [Once] I was totally redressed by one of my male colleagues right in front of everybody, calling me stupid and incompetent. It was uncalled for. It was one of those incidents where you go into your office, close the door, and try to compose yourself and not completely fall apart. Finally I confronted him. I said, "You know what? I cannot believe that you as a father of two daughters hold women in such low esteem. I really feel sorry for those girls because at least I had my father who was very supportive of me. Already you are setting them on the path where they are not going to be able to fully achieve their destiny and their goals because of how you felt about them and how you treated them and other women, because I'm sure you're not a differentiator."

As a woman in a "man's" profession she received virtually no positive mentoring as she worked her way up the organization. Indeed, she found that many of the managers became negative mentors. They not only did not help her, they discouraged her progress and demeaned her. Rather than becoming discouraged, Case used the negative mentoring she was receiving as data for ways NOT to manage and lead. Thus she turned what, for most women, are negative experiences that become detrimental to their careers into learning experiences from which she could develop her own leadership style as antithetical to these non-mentors.

The one saving grace of having gone through all this is that it made me very determined to mentor the people who came after me. Over time I built a team of brilliant women and men who took the company to new levels. Standing up for your people and building a respectful environment for both males and females helped change the course of how women were regarded and rewarded in our business.

In developing her own leadership style, Case turned the practices of discrimination into positive inclusive behaviors.

One of the biggest challenges for leadership today is a multi-generational issue. You can't use the same old approach anymore because in order to lead you really have to understand what is meaningful to the people you're leading. You have to understand that the values and needs of today's generation can be vastly different from the baby boomers....Different generations have different

*es on what they want in their lives. They want more balance, for
They don't want work, work, and more work. They also have a
___ent view of authority. They feel that the boss can be and should be
challenged, so you have to embrace these differences with an open mind.*

*Gone are the days of undisputed chain of command. Now you have to really
work with each individual person whom you need and who is really critical to
your operation. It's much trickier because you have to somewhat adapt to
that person, while maintaining your authority. For example, you can't
just get up there and give fight speeches because they don't resonate with a
multi-generational team. When you look around the room, you need to note
what perks up some people and who are shaking their heads saying, "Yeah,
we're just totally lost." You have to adapt your style to different types of people.
So I strive to make my leadership inclusive, so everyone gets the message...
however, they need it delivered.*

This leadership style makes for a very communicative company and
Case would be the first to tell you that while at FRB she promoted that
ideology to her staff, helping or mentoring those around them to become
better leaders. Indeed, one of the ways she evaluates leadership is by
identifying a person who is willing to undertake that process. As she says,
it requires courage and self-awareness to actually help someone who could
be a potential threat to you down the line. She likes people who "push the
envelope" and would rather encourage the one who pushes the boundaries
rather than someone who is complacent with the status quo.

A DIFFERENT KIND OF CEO: LEARNING THE JOB AND MAKING IT HER OWN

Even though she successfully rose to the top of FRB, Case has known very
uncertain times in her profession, particularly in the last few years of
dot-com blow-ups, the aftermath of 9/11, and some of the worst market
conditions in memorable history. A third of the business was lost when the
dot-coms blew up. Indeed, being part of a very large worldwide conglomer-
ate has its downside—the turmoil of companies in the group being bought
and sold, merged and demerged, changing personnel, and shifting
geographical economic environments. But she contends that it is only when
people have gone through a struggle for survival in such bleak circumstances that they come out with a unique education and a very different feeling
than merely experiencing robust markets. It completely changes the way
people feel, and act, and can create an enormous sense of loyalty. Case is also
quick to point out that survival requires a high degree of emotional intelligence. When a company is struggling, the leader has to be more self-aware,
have a sense of humor and real empathy coupled with a large dose of
optimism even in the face of disaster. None of these can be bluffed.

Case found that being a mentor or role model was a great responsibility.

I think you really have to understand how impactful you are on people, actively or passively. When you walk into an office or walk into a room, your very mood, or the very way you question a person, can determine a positive or a negative outcome. It took me a while to realize that when I became president, I was no longer "one of the guys." That was not what my staff wanted. Sure, they were looking for somebody down to earth, and who could see the humorous side of a situation. More importantly they were looking for a leader, someone they could trust and admire. So I think it's a very serious role to undertake.

Case contends that she never wanted to be a CEO and certainly does not relate well to celebrity CEO types.

There was no way that I was ever groomed to be a leader. I wasn't ever interested in being a CEO.

It is definitely a lonely job as concerns or fears often cannot be expressed to colleagues. The emotional recognition of difficult roles and decisions hardly ever moves upstream. The goal is to keep everyone else emotionally stable and focused.

Actually when you assume the role of a President/CEO it is one of the loneliest places that you could possibly be, because you really can't express your concerns and your fears to the degree that it would alarm other people. And I also discovered that even those in your inner circle can have a hard time because they have their own issues. It's really not their job to ask, "How can I lift this burden from you?" It just doesn't happen that way. That kind of emotional recognition of your difficult role seldom moves upstream. So your job is to keep everybody emotionally stable and focused, but don't count on others to realize that the need goes the other way. That is just the nature of the job.

To this end, like her father, Case relies heavily on her personal values and embedded these principles in her leadership at FRB. She fully supports meritocracy and firmly opposes entitlement—both of which take constant vigilance to enforce in an organization. She was raised to believe that you earn respect and promotion and are accountable for your destiny. A highly motivated individual, she has a real "can do" attitude and a realistic evaluation of obstacles. Taking over an organization entrenched in a paternalistic culture and a "job for life" mentality was a daunting challenge. Case has had to make some very difficult decisions on restructuring the company to ensure its very survival. As her company became part of a large public holding group, her staff had to understand that they were now playing by different rules in much more stringent times.

Case saw the company through an extremely harrowing period and she now wants to watch FRB thrive and see the people she helped develop take the company to new levels. Case's principal motivating factor through all the mayhem was to focus on the people who gave so much of their energy and intellectual capital to FRB and the practice of investor relations.

On the subject of leadership, Case has some sound advice regarding leading an organization from the front. She considered it her duty to develop people who might take over her job and she tried to recognize stars that may outshine her. This kind of attitude takes a lot of self-confidence and self-awareness and that is how she picked out future leaders at FRB—people who are fearless about nurturing others, even though some day, the people they mentor may become better, quicker, and smarter than themselves. She always tried to be fair and to be constantly accessible to her team. An open door policy and "walking the halls" help engender communication and trust. Case also worked hard at not creating conflicting actions by encouraging collaboration on decisions and seeking different opinions. To reach this point it is important to solicit ideas that may invite criticism, and one has to be prepared for that. The key is to create a challenging but respectful culture. It is not all easy though, and one of the hardest things in business is to stimulate and encourage creative thinking from your people. A CEO should never make the assumption that their employees are totally willing to share ideas, or even believe it is part of their job.

> *I like to invite opinions, I like to invite different points of view, I like to hear my viewpoint challenged, and I feel really good about acknowledging people who share their ideas. One of the hardest things in business is make certain that your people are not on autopilot. That means they are not thinking about how to do things better, how to apply some of the critical input that they receive from clients to improve the overall product and service offering. You have to encourage this kind of creative and critical thinking all the time. It was one of my biggest challenges, so when somebody says, "here's why we should consider doing it this way"...that feels like a victory. You won't get to that point unless you invite ideas and when you invite ideas you invite criticism, you invite a lot of other things, and you've got to be able to take it and use it positively.*

Case enjoyed building the company's reputation and successful careers for herself and those around her. She describes FRB as being alive with promise and her goal was to fulfill that promise both professionally and personally.

At the pinnacle of her career, it must be easy to feel that there is nothing new to learn but one resource Case has tapped into is a global organization of CEOs called Vistage International. Meeting once a month, it consists of people from all different backgrounds and is rather like having one's own personal advisory board. Any issue can, and is, confidentially discussed including outsourcing, exit strategies, and life balance. In addition, each member has personal one-on-one coaching for a couple of hours a month where confidential issues can be talked through. This strong network has also proven to be a great help from a personal standpoint.

Case found it extremely valuable and has made some very supportive friends through it.

For Case, every day was a different challenge and she stayed until it was time to leave. Her mantra is that when you feel a sense of completion, it is time to move on and give other people a chance to become leaders.

Real leaders always take the risk of helping somebody along who is potentially going to supplant them. But that is what it is all about. You cannot lead forever, you cannot live forever.

REFERENCE

Indvik, Julie. 2004. Women and leadership. In *Leadership theory and practice,* ed. Peter Northouse. 3rd ed. Thousand Oaks, CA: Sage Publications.

Chapter 8

Balancing Business and Family in the Difficult World of Finance: Adela Cepeda

Being an investment banker and having children is difficult. The time commitment is huge, and so that's an obstacle.

Adela Cepeda is an unusually talented woman who balances her financial expertise with her deep dedication to her family. Despite a number of significant obstacles including being a Latina in an almost all white-male business, widowhood, and a family of three children, she has successfully created her own municipal financial advisory firm (A.C. Advisory, Inc.) and a full-service brokerage company (ALTA Capital Group) while bonding with and inspiring her three daughters to do well.

EARLY CAREER OBSTACLES: FACING THE CHALLENGE OF DISCRIMINATION

One of the significant challenges for women and men today is balancing work and family. It is always a temptation for women with financial resources to leave the workplace. For those without other means this is not a choice. According to data gathered by a recent study, low-wage workers often have less control over their work–family choices, less flexible work schedules, and fewer opportunities to move to other more flexible job opportunities (Perlow 1998). Staying at home as an unpaid family "worker" is important and often is undervalued in our economy (Cepeda 1995, 4). Cepeda was fortunate not to have faced those economic and educational challenges. Still, balancing work and family demands is taxing in any circumstance. Cepeda chose a career, an ever-changing career, in the financial service industry, not easy, and with family responsibilities, more difficult. In the beginning, however, she did not see these work–family issues as obstacles, but rather as challenges to be met and dealt with.

Adela Cepeda

She saw her obstacles not as work–family conflicts, but because she was a Latina woman.

> *An obstacle I faced in that business where I started and spent the first decade of my profession was that being a woman, a young woman, and a Latina woman, I think, but mostly it was being a young woman, it was very hard to do the marketing. Because we were marketing, back then, to 55-year-old Chief Financial Officers, mostly white males, and—I'm not kidding—[on a marketing call] I would bring a young male associate to carry the books and bring him out for exposure and the client would turn and talk to the associate....That happened not just once. It happened in my own dinner club here in Chicago, where every time I went, they would give the bill to my male client. This happened over and over. I was fairly young, I started at twenty-two, right out of college, but this is the kind of business where after a few years if you understand the business, you have to generate revenue, and I was never in a strong position for that. Today, it's different. There are a lot more women in Treasury and in Chief Financial Officer positions. I would get attention today, but back then I did not. But I wanted to follow the career path of financial services. I didn't want to fall behind, and it was very hard.*

Cepeda's parents and four siblings emigrated from Colombia when she was a child, leaving behind a thriving family business. From the beginning Cepeda, as the oldest, was given the role as the exemplar for her siblings.

So really since I was a little girl, I've been trying to set an example—first for my sisters, and now for my daughters. I also recognize that, in the Latino community in general, there are not a lot of people with my educational skills, and with the opportunities that I've had. And that's an obligation, to set a high level of behavior, because I'm always featured in things, so I do think about that. I mean, I want to do the right thing. I don't seek out publicity, but when I agree to interviews and things like that, it's because there are so many negative stereotypes—especially of the Latina woman. Our stereotypes, I would say, if they're not negative, they're not exactly the most serious business image. We don't have it—we're always viewed as pretty, and we can dance, and are nice, but there isn't a vision of us as driven, professional women.

As the family exemplar, Cepeda attended Harvard University, graduating with honors, and received an MBA from the University of Chicago. Her experience at Harvard was life-changing.

I started at Harvard, and I think that it had a profound impact on me. First of all I never felt discriminated there. On the contrary I was accepted. Number two, I could try to do whatever I wanted there....Everything that was available seemed to be available to everyone. I never felt anything but opportunity at Harvard....That's where I lost my fear of achievement, or of failure. I lost my fear of failure [at Harvard], so that had a tremendous impact on me.

FOUNDING HER OWN BUSINESS: THE OPPORTUNITY AND FLEXIBILITY OF WOMEN'S ENTREPRENEURSHIP

Her earliest ambition was to run a large company such as IBM or AT&T or even a large financial institution. Entering the AT&T management program she thought concretely about how she might achieve such an end. Today she sees her small business as her best option given her family and difficulties finding a fit in the corporate world. Although she is enormously qualified and became vice president of corporate finance at Smith Barney, she concluded that there were more opportunities in a small firm than in corporate finance. She blames this partly on her personal restrictions on travel, but obviously being a Latina probably played a role as well. Cepeda has always combined family and career. Her career is as a means to work, and to remain intellectually challenged, but she has never prioritized that over creating time for her children.

Given those two commitments and her challenges as a Latina in a large firm, Cepeda, with two partners, started Abacus Financial Group in 1991. In 1995 Cepeda started her own business, A.C. Advisory, Inc., leading that company to become a significant player in municipal financing. Interestingly, she claims that her entrepreneurial spirit comes from Latina women. In Colombia, as in many parts of Latin America, vast numbers of women become entrepreneurs, making and selling all sorts of items in order to survive.

When I used to go frequently [to Colombia], and this was a long time ago, they would always ask us to bring an Oster blender because Oster was the best brand. They would set up these Oster blenders, or a Singer sewing machine, and they would make ice cream from their home and sell it. They would make milk shakes and sell them. It became a capital good that they would generate income from. And when you go to Mexico, you see that. When you go to Latin America, you see women in the street selling anything—things they make. Our culture is extremely entrepreneurial. It may be just survival-driven but it is also part of the culture. I don't know about the genetics of it, but it's doing something that I saw people do always. It's not degrading to be trying to sell. So I think that to elevate that, because of the opportunities that America has given me here, to the different role that I play now negotiating with Wall Street firms is worthwhile. And it is taking advantage of my economics studies and my finance MBA, but it's not really something foreign really. I want other people to know, other young women to know, that you can do it. You take what you learn and you apply it to a different set of facts, to a different environment. But there's nothing that you cannot do, if you have to do it.

LEADING WITH COURAGE AND INTEGRITY: SHAPING THE ORGANIZATION'S VISION

One of the lessons from Cepeda's leadership style is her developed sense of fearlessness. As she says, *I think a lot of achieving is your own fear—it is not letting your own fear limit you.* As a Latina woman at Harvard, University of Chicago, and then working in a large corporation, Cepeda had to learn not to be fearful despite sometimes being ignored or not getting the same opportunities as her more traditional colleagues. This enabled Cepeda to start several businesses with no thought of failure. She created herself as a person who could achieve as much as any of her contemporaries, and with that optimism and dauntless self-esteem, she was able to do just that. Her greatest achievement to date is when her firm was chosen as an advisor to New York City's financial team in the municipal bond issues. This was an enormous accomplishment for a relatively small Midwest firm and reflects Cepeda's intellectual ability and solid financial background that brought her firm to the attention of New York City.

Another lesson to be gleaned from Cepeda's career is her extraordinary self-confidence, despite obstacles, which allows her to admit her lack of knowledge on a certain subject. *When you are confident, you also know to say you don't know. . . . instead of giving wrong answers, you admit that. It is just better than to try to pretend.* Cepeda's strong knowledge base and her commitment to self-confidence and honesty enable her companies to develop trust and loyalty with their clients. This has allowed many of her clients in the bond markets to get "triple A" ratings, the highest rating in that financial area.

One time I told a client that they had paid too much for something. They had not asked me ahead of time, but I believed that whatever they got was more than market [value.] The client wanted us to write a letter saying that this was the best investment. I wouldn't do it. . . . I remember being asked three times, and I said "no." That municipality is still a client, and I never gave them that letter.

Cepeda has two other foci in her life. As a single mother of three children, she does not dismiss the importance of family and sees herself as a role model for her daughters. Setting an example, of course, can be trying at times, as she admits. Her other focus is to serve on several boards where her input can make a difference. As she says, *I feel a lot of responsibility. I have been given opportunities, and I should give back. That I feel a lot—giving back.* One of these is the Chicago Community Trust, a nonprofit organization that addresses the city's needs and needy. She chairs their investments and sees her contribution as making sure the investments are bringing in the best return for the Trust.

Cepeda's companies reflect her values—of knowledge development, honesty, trustworthiness, and giving back. One of her mantras is that her firms should keep abreast of any new ideas or trends, and she hires only those that are committed to this mission. Cepeda works hard to make sure her colleagues see themselves as that—colleagues, not employees, whose decisions make a difference to clients and to the company.

Cepeda admits to being motivated by a hope for recognition of her integrity and experience. She likes to influence the organizations she works with, both for charity and in for-profit companies. But she does not equate influence with power. Rather, influence comes from knowing what you are doing and linking that to helping organizations achieve their goals. She is also not reticent to help others. . . . *if they happen to be women, better, and if they happen to be Latinos, better, and if they happen to be minorities, triple better.*

Cepeda's vision for her companies, for the organizations whom she serves, and by analogy for her family, is that *the ideal organization [and the ideal family] is productive, and creates a positive environment for those in it, and for those working in it.* Thus, Cepeda sees her companies, her family, and her work with charities as linked with this consistent vision and commitment.

REFERENCES

Cepeda, Adela. 1995. Reward for raising kids is women who retire poor. *Crain's Chicago Business* 18 (36): 13.

Perlow, Leslie A. 1998. Boundary control: the social ordering of work and family time in a high-tech corporation. *Administrative Science Quarterly* 43: 328–57.

Chapter 9

The For-Profit Company with the Not-For-Profit Soul: Alison Chung

I am certainly pleased with our business results, but I am most proud of our team spirit and ethics, the focus on something bigger than our own personal self-interest, and the way we are able to deliver excellent service to our clients.

The word "career" is defined by Merriam-Webster as the "pursuit of consecutive progressive achievement especially in public, professional, or business life" (Merriam-Webster 2007). And as the word's Latin root "carrus," or car, implies, a career progresses along a road, on a journey. Siri Terjesen takes the analogy one step further and suggests that when an individual's journey leads to entrepreneurship, it is the culmination of the "embedded career capital" the entrepreneur has gathered along the road that leads one to success (Terjesen 2005).

Terjesen found that senior women are increasingly leaving corporate jobs to form their own ventures, relying on the "accumulations of the knowledge, skills, relationships, and networks when starting and growing new ventures" (Terjesen 2005). Alison Chung leveraged her varied and strategic career experience and contacts in building and expanding her entrepreneurial venture, TeamWerks.

Alison Chung is the President of TeamWerks, a full-service technology consulting firm which she founded in 1997. She took the experience she gained throughout her career at three large, prestigious firms and decided to go it alone with this capital as a foundation. Her strong sense of integrity, ethics, and the importance of creating a corporate culture based on values were her driving forces.

Although Chung credits her University of Chicago MBA degree with providing a solid grounding in business concepts, she confesses that her path to building a business was far from textbook entrepreneurship:

Alison Chung

I did not have a solid business plan, to be perfectly honest . . . the [University of Chicago] MBA program taught us to have these major business plans [and] to have a budget and growth projections for the next five years, but I really didn't. Because what was important to me was freedom—that would be priceless. If I could set forth our own culture and our values, it didn't matter to me if the company had two people, thirty people, fifty people, or one hundred people. That was what was important to me—to get together a group of people with similar values and similar goals.

After graduating with a master's degree in Mathematics from Stanford University, Chung was hired by IBM as a programmer. She started business school and continued her employment with IBM, but the lack of client interaction did not fit Chung's personality. A headhunter put her on a new professional course:

IBM is a great company, especially when you're young, in your 20s, and want to learn a lot. It has good corporate governance; it has good managers; it instills good values; it emphasizes respect for the individual, all of which I treasure to this day. So IBM provided a really good experience, but I was young when the headhunter called and said, "Would you like to be in a consulting environment? We have an opportunity for you and it's going to be glamorous."

The job was with PwC (PricewaterhouseCoopers), one of the "Big 6" consulting firms in 1986 when she started. *Of course I was tempted. I thought,*

"[A] good, glam job, why not? I'll be consulting, traveling, the whole thing," so I said yes. Her strong computer skills landed her on a technology engagement. *I envisioned New York, LA...and they said, "You are going to be at the prisons up in Illinois."...I said, "I must have misunderstood...somebody said glam. This doesn't sound very glam to me!"* Chung was incredulous but finally managed to adjust her initial expectations.

For the next two years, she traveled to the Illinois prisons every Sunday to create a trust fund system to manage inmates' income, returning home every Saturday for a brief weekend reprieve. During this time she earned a reputation for being a very hard worker. *I knew what the metrics were for success: the billable hours, the quality of the job...so I was the highest billable person in the entire office because I was constantly working [at the prisons]. I couldn't do anything else but bill. I was on the fast track, and I was promoted to manager very quickly.*

Chung completed her role on the prisons engagement and was assigned to one of the top five largest law firms in Chicago to conduct an assessment of the technology there—what little existed in the late 1980s. After just a few months in the role, the managing partner asked Chung to leave PwC to automate the entire law firm as the CIO (Chief Information Officer). She explains her decision to leave PwC:

> *So the temptation came again. The temptation was to stay in town, no more traveling, and so after several weeks I agreed. The project was very attractive—the fact that this large law firm did not have any computers, that I would be able to build everything from scratch, I would be able to link up their clients, I would be able to install e-mail [systems], create custom application programs for them, seemed very attractive.*

Chung was one of the early adopters of technology at the law firm and stayed there for almost ten years, but the division between the lawyers and the staff eventually led to her decision to move on professionally.

> *I realized that even though they appreciated me very much, and I loved my job, I would never be looked at the same way as the Partners looked at each other, or as they looked at the Associates, because I didn't have that J.D. And even if I had had ten Ph.D.'s, it would have been the same.*

Additionally, Chung had now experienced three different company cultures: IBM, PwC, and the large law firm, and she was always uneasy with the strong emphasis on the bottom line. While she recognized that a focus on profitability was central to the success of any business, Chung felt that it compromised her personal ethical and moral code. *I knew that I could not continue [at the law firm] forever and that the only way I could change my environment was to start something myself.*

The theory of values-based leadership provides a label for the culture Chung was seeking. Values-based leaders combine personal values and ethics with commercial sustainability in leading a business. The emphasis on the bottom line is balanced with the firm's reputation, social responsibility, and employee retention (Ancrum 2006/2007).

Chung left on good terms, with plenty of advance notice. She maintains a strong relationship with the law firm, a TeamWerks client to this day. She left intending to do the same type of work she was doing at the law firm [providing information technology (IT) services], but as an independent company.

NEW BUSINESS SEEKING CLIENTS

Chung's decision to start her own business was primarily motivated by the disconnect between her personal values and the values that she saw in the other organizations she had observed. *I decided [that] if I can't change [the business] then I just have to create my own.* So Chung and her partners, two Senior Managers from the law firm, formed their new venture and waited for business to start pouring in. It was slow going in the beginning. *[My partners and I] looked at each other and said, "Well, where are the clients?"* Since neither Chung nor her partners had any marketing experience, they decided that they needed to proactively find a client. To start, they responded to a "Request for Proposal" for IT work from the CPS (Chicago Public Schools). The fact that TeamWerks is a woman-owned business was very helpful in the proposal process. Chung was ultimately awarded the contract.

Despite this early triumph, Chung felt as though she had "gone into early retirement." The pace at CPS and the law firm represented the two ends of the spectrum. Instead of giving in to the new pace, she went to the CIO at the CPS and offered to read a new publication discussing the availability of federal money for putting technology into the schools. The CIO was happy to hand over the job of reading the publication, which was several thousand pages long. Chung read the report, applied on behalf of the CPS, and received an award for $55 million. When the award was announced Chung joked with the CPS CIO: *My [original] contract cost $50,000 and I got you $55,000,000. Could there be a better return?* The award also represented a turning point for TeamWerks. The CIO was so grateful that he offered the implementation work to TeamWerks, requesting that Chung hire four more employees and partner with the large vendors that work with CPS, including IBM.

Chung's prior contacts through IBM and the law firm also helped her build the business in the early years. *The business grew organically, and while this was going on, we were receiving calls from a number of law firm contacts. You will notice how I always say, "We got called," because there's no active marketing. To this day, we don't market our services.*

Another major turning point for TeamWerks came when Chung's team was asked to investigate a computer forensics issue for a health care institution. Chung combed through two hundred boxes of computer code and three weeks later she found the information she needed to answer the questions her client had asked. The client was so impressed with Chung's research that he asked her to testify on the institution's behalf in front of the IRS the following day.

> *[The IRS lawyers] said, "Who's that girl over there?" and [our lawyers] said, "That's our expert." And the investigators said, "Gentlemen, this is going to be a quick day."*

Chung proved them wrong, assisted by her photographic memory for numbers. Her testimony was flawless and the panel of investigators was shocked.

> *The questions stopped. We won the case. Our client gained [a] $50,000,000 write-off, and then it became an addiction. Some people go to Las Vegas for relaxation; I often testify for fun—I don't mean that I take it lightly at all, I simply love the adrenaline rush.*

What used to be a burden (she still remembers license plates she glanced at when she was four years old) is now the basis for a profitable aspect of her growing business.

Chung's success in computer forensics and litigation was only beginning. To this day, TeamWerks has never been on the losing side of a matter that went to trial. This is a great source of pride for Chung and the employees of TeamWerks, especially since this is a rare assertion to be able to make in the field. TeamWerks recently represented the second largest software company in the world and won a preliminary injunction for it after two-and-a-half years of proceedings. *That was one of the largest cases ever, in the history [of this field]—and for us, a small company, to be involved and to be able to assist in winning. That was a big deal for me.*

THE SECRET TO SUCCESS: HIRING THE RIGHT PEOPLE

So what is the secret to all of this success? Chung says she is always asked if there is a specific business model or a framework for her company's continued success.

> *I look at them and say, "No, it's very simple…you simply adhere to the truth. That's it. You do not bend the data to suit the day. Where there's a gray area you don't push it over the line and make it a white or a black. It is gray and you say that it's gray."*
> *I think some people, for a variety of reasons, including that they think they're being loyal to their clients, try to push things, and that's where it gets bad. Once you push it over the line there's no turning back. Once you pass the point of being 100% truthful, there's no return. We will not cross that line— nobody in this company crosses that line. That is one of the most serious things that I consider when I hire people.*

TeamWerks looks for much more than just a skilled candidate when it makes a hiring decision. Prospective employees must go through a rigorous screening process to be sure that they truly possess this ethical and value-based core that Chung has worked so hard to establish at TeamWerks. She describes it as a strong sense of integrity:

> When I hire people, or when my HR manager hires people, we look for the obvious: they have to be talented; they have to have degrees in computer science. But beyond that, during the course of our interview we are actively looking to see whether [the candidate's] values include that something that shows they're looking for more in life than self-interest. That is extremely and exceptionally important to me and to my two Principals.

Once hired, Chung interacts with every employee on a regular basis to be sure that they all understand the direction of the firm and their place in achieving the organizational goals. Her employees have proven their commitment to the greater organization through their loyalty and dedication. To illustrate the lengths to which employees go for the clients, Chung tells the story of an employee who handled an emergency situation via cell phone while standing up in a wedding:

> Not only did he return the call, because it was a situation with one of the client's files, [but] he called his mother who took a personal day in order to drive the tape down [to the office]. Nobody asked him to do that. Nobody. I did not ask him to do that, my managers did not ask him, but I guess this is an example as to how grateful I am that my employees see what is necessary—what the critical success factors are to make us competitive in the marketplace, to maintain our niche—and they do whatever it takes without ever being asked. I think I have effectively communicated our values because their actions show that they're very committed.

In a service industry such as TeamWerks, where employee behavior and expertise represents the "product" to clients, this is one way for companies to safeguard their reputation. Another way is to foster a culture where employees uphold the values of the firm at all costs. A recent article on leadership proposes, "If all employees see themselves as leaders, as guardians of the values, and if they see that even small acts can be leadership acts if properly handled, the company will be more united in protecting its basic beliefs" (Cohen 2001).

SHARING THE WEALTH: GIVING BACK IN THE COMMUNITY

TeamWerks has done many things in an effort to support the community and its clients such as CPS, including investing much of its profits in giving back. For example, TeamWerks runs a summer camp for CPS children.

We do it because we really believe in it. There are a lot of kids who go to the Chicago Public Schools who don't get to go to camp because they don't have the financial resources to do so. We hired a teacher who coached them rigorously full time for one month—everything from golf to baseball to kayaking and bicycle riding.

Every day of the camp included a special event or activity and many TeamWerks employees participated. Chung believes that the time and money her organization commits to such endeavors help employees develop not only personally but professionally as well.

One of our clients once said that we are a for-profit company with a not-for-profit soul. . . . I want our employees to really feel driven in that way, because not only is it good for them to do not-for-profit work, it's good for the other work that they do [and] it shows through in the quality of that work. It shows through because they are not just doing it to rake in those billable hours; they are doing it because they really want to pursue excellence. They really want to see justice being served. They really want to do the best because they believe in something bigger than themselves. That is absolutely mandatory.

Chung not only provides opportunities for her employees to give back, but she also makes time to serve on community boards. In February 2007, Chung was selected to serve on the board of the Women's Business Development Center. She is also active in numerous professional and community associations in Illinois, especially organizations which promote educational and cultural growth.

THE POWER OF INFLUENCE

To Chung, being in a position of influence has many intangible benefits, including the peace of mind that turning away work which is inconsistent with the ethical code of the organization will not break the bank. In fact, she believes that the organization may be richer for making the right choices. Chung says,

I'm always focused on the quality of the client service, on doing what I think is right, on doing things that are not particularly driven by self-aggrandizement. But now that the business has grown and has established a reputation, I see how the engine works, and I see that it can be helpful to have the power and influence if you want to do things for the greater good. And the power, influence, and money all go hand in hand. That's how it's played. It's nice to have some of it. It's also nice not to be tempted into doing corrupt things when you have it, because then suddenly the doors open and you have a lot of opportunities that you didn't have before. I see other people being tempted and subsequently changing.

The power, influence, and profits that Chung has achieved are the result of her business savvy and strong leadership abilities; however, the "doing well by doing good" mission at TeamWerks is also the result of the early influences in Chung's life—both her family and educational experiences. Chung's father was a strong role model for her. He was a physician in Hong Kong and engaged in a great many philanthropic activities during his life. Her brother has followed in his footsteps. Both her father and brother have spent a lot of time providing free care to refugees in Hong Kong. *No one ever explicitly said, "this is the way you should live your life," but I think a lot of us learn from viewing what people do, not what they say.*

Chung's educational experiences also shaped her as a leader. She identifies her education at Wellesley College as one of the most important of these experiences.

> *It is such a haven for young women. We got to be in all these leadership roles that we never dreamed we would be in. It helped my confidence. [What I learned there] was not manifested until a lot later—my confidence and public speaking ability—because I still consider myself technical and not very eloquent. But once you have that foundation you always have it. You know that you can do anything that you want to do, that it's really up to you.*

Spiritual role models taught Chung to "see beyond self-interest" and to work for the greater good. *I admire the Dalai Lama [and] I admire Mother Teresa. Those are the people I look up to, and that's what I mean by "seeing beyond self-interest," because it is my belief that we are here for the greater good.* Although she doesn't ever discuss this in her business dealings, Chung believes that it is inherent to the way she conducts herself.

Chung also believes in the power of a positive mentor. She discusses her appreciation for another woman highlighted in this book, Desiree Rogers:

> *One of my best mentors is Desiree Rogers [of Peoples Gas and North Shore Gas]. I really admire Desiree a lot. [She] helped me so much, way before I became "successful" in the eyes of everybody else....She opened a lot of doors for me....When the public perceives that you are successful, all sorts of doors open, but that's not until they see that you are successful, not until they see that you are in the newspaper. Desiree did this for me way before anything happened, and I will be grateful to her for a long time.*

Chung returns the favor by mentoring others. She mentors a number of high school students from the CPS, as well as several business school students at the University of Chicago. *I think that it's part of our responsibility [to mentor]. I think it's a privilege [to be considered a role model]. It's an honor. Once again, I think that it's a responsibility. We owe it to the younger people to share what we have learned with them. I think we all share [a responsibility].*

DEFINING THE TEAMWERKS LEGACY

As Chung looks back at the tenure of the TeamWerk she reflects on her proudest accomplishment—the culture:

I am certainly pleased with our business results, but the proud team spirit, the ethics, the focus on something bigger than our own personal self-interest, and the way we are able to deliver excellent service to our clients, keeping all of that in mind.

So what attributes comprise the ideal organization in her eyes? *The ideal organization is one that brings out the best qualities in all of the individuals within the organization and has a synergistic effect to make it something a lot bigger than the individual parts.* With this in mind, Chung's hopes for the future of the business and the ultimate legacy of the organization are *to continue doing what it is that we're doing in terms of our business model and be privileged to be profitable enough to continue to help the younger generation and the students who lack the resources to further their own education. I think that would be so great.* Without a doubt, Chung has certainly brought a full meaning to the term "career."

REFERENCES

Ancrum, R. December 2006/January 2007. The principal's principles. *Financial Management* 57–58.

Cohen, D. January 2001. Who's minding the future? *Executive Excellence* 1 (18): 20.

Merriam-Webster. 2007. *Definition of career.* Retrieved March 17, 2007, from http://www.merriam-webster.com/dictionary/career.

Terjesen, S. 2005. Senior women managers' transition to entrepreneurship: Leveraging embedded career capital. *Career Development International* 3 (10): 246–59.

Chapter 10

Creating an Entrepreneurial Legacy Through Technology Education: Caroline Sanchez Crozier

You can have the vision, you can have the relationships, but if you're not going to have the resources to see it through, with people who have multiple strengths that complement yours, then you're not going to succeed.

Caroline Sanchez Crozier is the founder, CEO, and President of CSC Learning (CSC), a consulting company specializing in education and technology that was established in 1988. The firm provides innovative e-learning solutions specializing in scientifically based reading interventions for all learners to succeed. Crozier directs the company's business development and strategic relationships. Acknowledged widely as a leading visionary in the field of learning technologies, she has a strong commitment to quality, community service, and excellence in education.

IN PURSUIT OF THE AMERICAN DREAM

Crozier's life and work experiences reflect the American dream. She emigrated from Mexico with her family when she was only eight years old. They moved in pursuit of a better future, including the opportunity for all the children in the family to obtain a quality education. That goal was accomplished when Crozier became the first in her family to graduate from college in the United States by earning a bachelor's degree from Dominican University in 1979. She became a Certified Public Accountant in 1985, and held various financial positions in major corporations including Premark, McDonald's Corporation, Continental Bank, and Deloitte & Touche. After years of working experience as an accountant and a manager, she found, like many professional women,

Caroline Sanchez Crozier

that she was struggling to combine the dual roles managing her career and family.

Crozier decided to stay home with her small children, and to do projects on the side. It was through this experience that she observed the changes that were underway with school reform. For example, in the Chicagoland area, six hundred schools were managing their own budgets and making their own purchases.

She recounts,

I started by working for other small businesses. These were Hispanic-owned businesses in the area of cable television, performing contracted work. These first had a goal of recruiting women, and I met with several businesses doing work with the schools. I was hired immediately, for approximately ten hours per week. I was exposed to a whole new world, from corporate to small business consulting. I was able to wear many hats. One of the projects responded to demands of this new school reform. I was fascinated by it, and for the first time, women had an advantage. If you were a Hispanic woman you could get all kinds of contracts. I was home with my 2-year-old and my newborn.

I started handling a lot of other things, such as sales calls, and the work was computer-related, so I had to learn myself.

She knew she could respond to the needs of the school reform movement, and began to network.

Six months into it, I was working 30 hours per week consulting with a business where not everything was going in the direction I would have liked to have seen. I decided to break away and do my own consulting. It happened over a weekend.

During that weekend, she took the steps necessary to be incorporated, and later became certified as a woman-owned enterprise. Minority businesses—such as Hispanic or women-owned—were given preferential treatment when contracts were awarded and, being reasonably priced, school managers were quick to hire her. The more work she did in education, the more Crozier was committed to pursuing her own business.

THE LAUNCH OF CSC: CONNECTING TECHNOLOGY TO EDUCATIONAL COMMUNITIES

She formed CSC in 1988 as a technology and education firm, and in a short span of five years, the company grew from one person to twenty people. The beginning was very challenging, as Crozier recalls,

I was going into a new world with a lot of uncertainty, and a lot of unknowns. It was fascinating to go into schools and provide resources, and try to make a difference in education. I was an immigrant. I was the first in my family to graduate from college and have a profession, and I felt I could make a difference and contribute to my community through my business technology resources. I was learning about this while I was running a business, because at that time technology was new to everybody.

The formation of CSC reflects the high growth of small businesses in technology-related industries. The Small Business Administration's Office of Advocacy published a report that estimates that approximately 60% of high-growth small private firms were in services, and that industries that are more technically oriented are more accommodating to small fast-growing private firms (Eckhardt and Shane 2006).

As is common during the early launch period of any new business, there was a lot of unfamiliar territory and uncertainty. Buoyed by the support of her family, Crozier proceeded energetically ahead by introducing emerging technologies to schools and trying to make a difference in education. Crozier made the focus of her business the provision of technology, computers, and services to schools with Apple Computer, Inc. as her main partner. She enjoyed the exposure her new position gave her. Working with small businesses, she learned to wear many hats. Working in the computer industry, Crozier learned to respond quickly to change. When asked what helped her grow the business, she described the importance of having a focus, and driving the growth of the company toward the achievement of those focal goals:

> *I think growth depended on having the vision to move forward and to respond to the never-ending changes. Along the way I've tried different things, but ultimately having a focus where you can make it, where you're uniquely positioned—your competitive advantage [is key]. Over the years, we've added different experience, different resources, and I think we have a unique position in this marketplace. So, I would say being visionary about putting all those pieces together is where we come in and have something unique to offer.*

In some ways, Crozier was fortunate because the market opportunity was unfolding and the niche was expanding as CSC was forming. She had tremendous support and resources within her own family. As her young brothers and sisters came out of college, Crozier's father made sure that they helped their sister out in her new business. Some of them still work with her today, twenty-five years later!

There were obstacles along the way. CSC had to be in a position to be able to bid for a contract knowing that they would not be paid for more than six months. As Crozier says,

> *A contract is one thing, but getting paid is quite another. You have to have deep pockets and resources. I had none of that. The biggest challenge is capital, but because of my background as an accountant, I was comfortable with numbers and having a conversation with bankers. I had the plan to the point where I thought people would listen and understand. I recommend that, especially to women. Go to your local bank and build a relationship with them. I went to the president who listened to my needs: "sweat equity." He stood by me and guided me. Big banks wouldn't do that. He is still my banker today.*

Marketplace and other environmental changes, however, were outside of her control. When CSC was born, Apple Computers was its main partner, and at that time, Apple had an 80% share of the marketplace. Then Microsoft arrived and the rest, as they say, is history. Overnight, most of Apple's dealers went out of business, but CSC survived. Even though revenues were cut back by 80%, Crozier, ever the visionary, had looked at ways of diversifying, and the company's educational programs and services carried them forward. Nevertheless, it was an immense struggle and all the company's capital had to be reinvested back into training and resources because their main income channel changed overnight. This is a hurdle that many small businesses would not have been able to overcome, yet with Crozier's persistence and strong leadership, CSC survived and thrived.

CSC's core competencies include supplemental reading resources (K–Adult), assessments, instructional software, professional development consultation, cognitive development software, bilingual/ESL programs (Spanish–English), professional development, tutoring services, and training and technical services. CSC's extensive client list includes the U.S. Department of Labor, Chicago Public Schools, City Colleges of Chicago, City of Chicago, Sun Microsystems, and Unisys (Gundry and Kickul 2007).

Crozier described two criteria she considers important for success:

One is finding something unique where you can position and have an advantage in terms of the programs and services [and] in terms of effectiveness. The second one is the relationships that you've established and continue to establish—where it's a personal connection where they're not just buying your program, but they're putting their faith in you and what you can deliver based on what you offered. So it really comes down to a personal commitment that you make. That is something that I address up front with the people that hire me, or boards that I'm on.

ON MENTORS AND MENTORING: RECEIVING SUPPORT AND GIVING BACK THROUGH COMMUNITY INVOLVEMENT

As mentioned earlier, Crozier's family moved to the United States from Mexico determined to live the American dream. Family has always been her prime concern. Crozier even moved nearer to her sister, who had offered to help raise Crozier's children while she built her business. Looking back, Crozier names her parents as two of her role models. Despite cultural traditions that were not as supportive of girls' higher education, Crozier said her mother was always very supportive. Her father worked in factories and had no formal education, but he had an entrepreneurial streak. It was very important to him that his children finish school and not experience the hardships he had known.

Crozier met her husband, Terry, in college, and over the past twenty-eight years, he has supported her in her entrepreneurial career, and eventually left his job thirteen years ago to join CSC as the company's Chief Operating Officer. Another mentor is a fellow school board president, in whom she saw a lot of similarities with respect to her career. He helped her along the way with many contacts, and her network began to expand.

Social relations play an important role in the establishment and growth of a new firm, and entrepreneurs use their social capital to access resources in each phase of the new business creation process (Greve and Salaff 2003). Social capital refers to connections with outside parties who provide access to a wide variety of resources.

Asked whether she sees herself as a role model or mentor, Crozier certainly tries to be there for others.

*I share my experiences. I share what I've gone through, and how I am still
in business. I feel good that I pursued a business degree. My clients are
schools and education has become a passion for me...helping youth reach
their potential.*

Volunteer work and giving back to the community are very important to
her and she sits on a number of committees and boards. She participated
in the Leadership Illinois Class of 2003 and is a member of the LULAC
(League of United Latin American Citizens), the largest and oldest Hispanic
organization in the United States, and of the National Education Commission. She is also a board member of the Hispanic Civic Committee of
Chicago and the Women's Business Development Center, as well as a trustee
of Dominican University.

She particularly praises the Women's Business Development Center as
one of the most successful nonprofit organizations supporting women
entrepreneurs in the country. Early on, the Center reviewed her business
plan for CSC, supported her, and made her feel that she was never really
alone. Through the Center, she was invited to the White House to receive
the prestigious Small Business Person of the Year Award in 1993 from
President Clinton.

Crozier has a strong commitment to quality, community service, and
excellence in education and workforce development. Education has become
a passion for her and, whenever possible, she works on initiatives that help
youth reach their potential. She has received numerous local and national
awards over the years and is currently State Education Chair for LULAC
of Illinois and sits on the Illinois Literacy Commission and the Chicago
Workforce Board.

The mission of the Workforce Board is to support the vision of Chicago as
a world-class city by ensuring the creation of a workforce development
system that sustains economic growth and competitiveness by meeting the
needs of employers for qualified workers and expanding employment
opportunities for Chicagoland residents. It provides a forum where
business, labor, education, government, community-based organizations,
and other stakeholders work together to develop strategies that can address
the supply and demand challenges confronting local business and industry.

Crozier is very active on civic boards and contributes her time and
expertise to support educational programs in Latino communities and
other underserved groups. In 1998 she initiated a model for a new Master
of Arts in Teaching and Technology for bilingual teachers at Dominican
University.

In 1999, Crozier established a tutoring model to support struggling
readers that uses research-based curriculum and software. As a result of
the program's success, CSC was approved as an "SES tutoring provider"
under the federal "No Child Left Behind Act," which funds private after-
school tutoring programs for K-12 education nationwide. In 2006 Crozier
founded CLEAR (Coalition of Latinos for Educational Advancement and

Representation) in Chicago to promote collaboration among Latino leaders and increase educational resources for the community at large.

COMMUNICATING THE VISION: BUILDING THE COMPLEMENTARY TEAM

Crozier expanded the company to a third division with e-learning solutions specializing in scientifically based reading interventions. CSC's educational consultants assist schools with the implementation of research-based online programs and software to help all students improve their academic achievement and learning potential. She is in current plans to establish an office in Mexico with Chris Cook, her longtime friend with a Ph.D. in educational psychology, who recently joined CSC as a vice president. It was Cook who almost twenty years ago gave her the first contract which inspired her to start CSC. They are now in the process of setting up a separate company to expand internationally.

Crozier cites her biggest accomplishment as providing the vision for moving forward in a changing environment and marketplace and in having people follow her vision. But, as she says, she couldn't have done any of it without her family. For Crozier, building partnerships with trust and sharing her philosophy are her reasons for working. And her mission statement says it all: "Connecting technology with teaching and learning to offer more opportunities to more individuals."

Her working style, however, includes no micromanagement. She is a participative leader. She has built up a team of people who internally manage the office and take care of her staff. She has a female Vice President of Operations who has been with the company for more than thirteen years and a brother and a sister who have been with CSC since day 1. As she explains,

> I realize my strengths are outside—conveying our work and making connections and partnerships. My work is more global and visionary and they all know that. Other people are best at doing the internal management. When we work with internal initiatives, we do brainstorming—it's a consulting process. We design a program around it, and we make sure we're on the same page and focused. Everybody has his or her roles. When we ask, "What is our vision for working on this project?"—I'm part of that. Once it's set, I'm looking for the next one.

With regards to power and influence, Crozier is satisfied if she can influence in a positive way:

> I don't have time to get sick, or think negatively for too long. You only have a finite amount of energy so don't use it negatively. You also have to be a positive thinker. You can have the vision, you can have the relationships, but if you're not going to have the resources to see it through, with people who

have multiple strengths that complement yours, then you're not going to succeed.

EDUCATING INTO THE FUTURE

Crozier is determined to keep doing what she is doing "...until I die." As long as she is driven to continue making a positive impact on education, she will continue. She is currently working with new schools as a result of Mayor Daley's Renaissance 2010. The fundamental goal of this initiative is to turn around Chicago's most troubled elementary and high schools by creating one hundred new schools in neighborhoods across the city over the next six years, providing new educational options to underserved communities, and relieving school overcrowding in communities experiencing rapid growth. A daunting challenge, but one that Crozier is especially suited not only to meet but to exceed.

There is so much I learned in education that has shaped my life. I'm a passionate person, trying to make the world a better place by the work I do. My legacy is to create a better place than I came from...to reach our potential as individuals. I see a lot of gaps in that area. My business has become a way of me achieving my goal. I do it with conviction.

REFERENCES

Eckhardt, J.T., and S. Shane. 2006. "Innovation in small business performance: Examining the relationship between technological innovation and within-industry distributions of fast-growth firms." *Small Business Research Summary, No. 272, March.* Small Business Office of Advocacy. http://www.sba.gov/advo/research/rs272.pdf (accessed March 10, 2007).

Greve, A., and J.W. Salaff. 2003. Social networks and entrepreneurship. *Entrepreneurship: Theory and Practice* 28 (1): 1–22.

Gundry, L.K., and J.R. Kickul. 2007. *Entrepreneurship strategy: Changing patterns in new venture creation, growth, and reinvention.* Thousand Oaks, CA: Sage Publications.

Chapter 11

A Servant Leader in Values and Actions: Deborah L. DeHaas

My roots are very much in client service. My job is all about helping other people be more effective in what they need to do in serving our clients.

SERVANT LEADERSHIP: A TRULY EMPOWERING VALUES-BASED STYLE

Servant leadership may be a key to empowerment, and several authors have noticed the connection between the two concepts. What is servant leadership? "Exemplary leaders use their power in service of others" and enable them to act by strengthening them and developing them into leaders (Kouzes and Posner 2003, 8). Greenleaf (1977) noted that a great leader is a servant first, and that the conscious choice of wanting to serve *first* makes one want to lead. The ultimate goal of a servant leader is fulfilling others' needs. Contrast this with the traditional style of leadership that emphasizes power and control. Servant leaders serve followers to promote their empowerment and enable them to accomplish organizational goals.

Dess and Picken (2000) have also noted that a great leader is a great servant. Servant leaders may be effective in providing keys to empowerment, such as flexible resources for employees, depending on their needs. For example, leaders may be coaches, listeners, or providers of information, if that is what is needed by their followers. Servant leaders also facilitate the growth of their employees, both professionally and emotionally. They enable others to discover their own inner spirit and potential to make a difference, and ultimately to develop into servant leaders themselves.

Deb DeHaas exemplifies servant leadership both inside and outside of the workplace, and the roots of this leadership style may be seen in her upbringing, and the values that were ingrained in her. She puts those values into practice while serving her employees, clients, and community.

Deborah L. DeHaas

THE FORMATION OF A SERVANT LEADER'S VALUES

DeHaas is not the sort of person to rest on her laurels. In 2004 she was named Midwest Regional Managing Partner of Deloitte & Touche USA LLP, where she also serves as Vice Chairman. As one of the big four global accounting groups in over 120 countries, the job is definitely not for the fainthearted! Prior to Deloitte, she was Managing Partner at Arthur Andersen and responsible for their strategic direction and client relations activities and was admitted to partnership in 1993. She welcomed her new position at Deloitte because *it gives me the opportunity to really impact what I'm passionate about—our clients and our people.*

The fast-paced life must be in her genes—her sister, Betsy Holden, was Co-CEO of Kraft until 2003 and President of Global Marketing and Category Development until 2005. She was also ranked Number 1 by women business leaders in the *Sun Times* 100 Most Powerful Women in Chicago in 2004—DeHaas was not far behind at Number 8 and together they are definitely Chicago's power sisters. It is fair to say that Holden, being four years older, certainly made an impression on the younger DeHaas who clearly benefited from her older sister as coach and mentor. DeHaas's mother was also extremely influential in giving her a taste for accountancy when she would wistfully relate her early days as an accountant at Gulf Oil. Clearly attracted to the occupation, DeHaas's career path was set.

Her mother's memories were instrumental in DeHaas's choice of careers. Equally important were the strong values that her parents instilled in her from an early age. *I remember my mother telling me that "you don't have to be the best, just do your best."* So early on she had the role models of her parents and siblings who all believed in honoring commitments and giving more than 100%.

Looking back on the highlights of her career, DeHaas is particularly proud to have been selected for the Crown Fellowship Program in 2002. It honors the memory of Chicago industrialist Henry Crown, whose legendary career was marked by a lifelong commitment to honor, integrity, industry, and philanthropy.

Each year, a class of twenty Crown Fellows is chosen from among young executives and professionals nominated for their potential to provide leadership at the highest levels of corporate and civic responsibility. The selected candidates already will have proved themselves and enjoyed considerable success in the private or public sector.

The program is a unique mix of intellectual and personal development exercises designed to broaden the perspectives of the participants and hone their values-based leadership and seeks to develop the next generation of community-spirited leaders. The program provides them with the necessary tools to meet the challenges of corporate and civic leadership in the twenty-first century.

It is clear that the two-year Crown program had a great effect on DeHaas. While on the program at the Aspen Institute, she developed powerful relationships with her class and has stayed in touch with a number of them since graduating in 2002. It continues her passion of lifelong learning and benefiting from the experiences of people outside of her normal "group," a concept she was first introduced to back at Duke University, her alma mater.

There is no doubt in her mind that the experience has changed the way she leads. She describes the program as an inspirational experience, having mixed with people who had achieved a phenomenal level of success in very different fields. DeHaas feels the program helped her to recognize the benefit of having key people around you that you trust and respect, as well as the importance of the leader seeking insights from a broad group of people who ultimately have the same types of ethics and values as yourself.

EMPOWERING EMPLOYEES AND SERVING CLIENTS: SERVANT LEADERSHIP IN ACTION

DeHaas is motivated by opportunities to make a difference and help impact people in a positive way. She likes to get the best out of her people. Her golden rules include being a good communicator with the people around you and treating people with dignity, respect and in a fair-minded way. She engages them in the consultative process and encourages them to come to conclusions that create solutions for the stakeholders. True to the servant leadership style, DeHaas helps the group find the best course of action, and in so doing helps others discover their potential to make a difference.

Always looking for opportunities to help mentor and develop her team, DeHaas has a very strong responsibility to help women be successful. She recalls Madeleine Albright saying "there's a special hell for women who don't help other women!" So DeHaas hopes that her team feels she is supportive as she helps them play different roles and encourages them to collaborate.

DeHaas describes herself as most effective with a team of people. She has always worked in an environment where there has been a team. In her view, you recruit the right people and build a great team around you, whose members recognize and embrace their roles. Goal-setting comes next; it is really critical to lay out what is trying to be accomplished and what happens if that goal is achieved.

Her biggest accomplishments have come from this strategy. At Deloitte, DeHaas works with a great team who help put together the strategies needed to respond to changing environments and they help to execute those strategies in a collaborative way. To her way of thinking, this approach brings together good people from many different parts of the organization— both clients and staff. She regards her industry as a simple business that only needs great people to service clients well. If it is also fun, then that is a bonus.

In a service environment, DeHaas believes that it is important to have a servant mentality. *I practice servant leadership and am here to serve people. My position at Deloitte has given me tremendous opportunity to help the service, because I am in a service business that helps to make things better for the client.* Unlike other leaders who are driven by huge power needs, servant leaders make a conscious choice to serve others first; that is their primary motivation for leading (Greenleaf 1977).

Her personal values include the need for alignment in her working goals. In any long-term career, there ultimately has to be a long-term relationship with the organization that promotes that thinking. Her core values include integrity, quality of client service, quality of people, and a strong commitment to everyone—clients and staff alike—in them wanting to be in the place where they work.

A SERVANT LEADER GIVES BACK TO THE COMMUNITY

One of my passions is community service. DeHaas was brought up in a small town south of Pittsburgh, and attended public school with kids whose parents worked in the area's steel mills and coal mines. *There was always the sense that we needed to give something back because we were extremely blessed* recalls DeHaas. She particularly remembers one incident when she and her siblings hosted a backyard carnival to fund-raise and collected $25.

Serving the community is in DeHaas's lifeblood. From her childhood and all through her career, client service and serving others has been her mantra so it comes as no surprise to learn that she and her husband teach Sunday school at their local church. She readily admits that her role as a leader at Deloitte has given her a tremendous opportunity to help her local business community—a particular passion.

In the past several years, there have been major shifts in the professional services landscape that would have been difficult to anticipate. However, these shifts have provided significant opportunities for people within the industry to grow and develop personally and professionally. DeHaas is convinced that some of these changes and obstacles gave her unique opportunities to help a number of her former colleagues at Andersen find something longer term in their career and help them make *soft landings.*

That strong philanthropic ethic lives on today as she helps to run several community fund-raising efforts. For almost seventy-five years, the United Way has been bringing people and resources together to improve lives within the community. It develops programs to fill social service gaps, advocates for policy change, and raises awareness about critical health and human service needs in metropolitan Chicago. It is a cause dear to DeHaas's heart because it creates long-term solutions that improve lives and build stronger communities by collaborating with schools, businesses, and the government among others.

DeHaas took on the leadership role of General Campaign Chair for the United Way Metro Chicago in 2003 and 2004. She was the first female campaign chair, and the only campaign chair to stay in the role for two years. During her tenure, there were major changes that took place, including a restructuring of the board and a merging of the organization to make it more efficient. This major transformation that took place within the charity when it was under her leadership strengthened the organization and stabilized fund-raising efforts. She has enjoyed it so much that she offered to stay on to help secure the United Way's future by serving as cochair of fund-raising for the Tocqueville Society, which is focused on gifts of amounts $10,000 and higher. She has also served as Vice Chair of the United Way Metro Chicago Board.

In addition to her commitment to the United Way, DeHaas served as cochair of the fund-raising committee for Chicago 2016, the organization dedicated to bringing the 2016 Summer Olympics to Chicago. In this role, she worked closely with a committee of fund-raisers to raise $25 million in private donations needed to finance Chicago's bid for the Olympics. Since Chicago was selected to represent the United States in the International Bid process, DeHaas will continue to be involved with Chicago 2016 to raise more money as Phase II of the Bid continues. DeHaas says the ability to help make a difference is one of the most gratifying things she gets to do. It is hard work but rewarding and fun and she is enjoying making a positive impact on the lives of many people.

MODELING BALANCE AT WORK AND AT HOME

Regarding herself, DeHaas likes to think that she is a role model. *Frankly I feel a responsibility to be a role model. I have this dream there's a point in time where there's not just one role model that people have in terms of what it takes to be successful.* Being in a highly visible role, she works hard to bring a high level of energy to most things that she does and is enthusiastic and committed.

Whether she is consciously aware of it or not, DeHaas clearly models her core values in the workplace, and as such serves to strengthen the organizational culture at Deloitte. Indeed, actions do speak louder than words, and this servant leader's actions are consistent with her values. It is crucial for culture formation and maintenance that a leader's spoken message and enacted message be congruent. As Schein (1985) noted, the primary means for changing and maintaining culture are the leader's roles of modeling, coaching, and reacting to critical incidents. Although the structures of organizations, and artifacts like the spoken and published mission statements, should also be congruent with the primary mechanisms, they are of secondary importance to the leader's role in organizational culture formation and maintenance. DeHaas not only strengthens followers through an empowering, servant leadership style, she has also been a strong role model and advocate for women with families, and demonstrates that in a supportive organizational environment, women can have it all. However, as will be seen below, it was not always like this at Deloitte.

DeHaas's first position was as a staff auditor position with Andersen, then Chicago's largest accounting firm. Apart from loving the job, she also met her husband there. DeHaas made partner at Andersen in 1993 and went on to have three sons. She says she never considered not having children to further her career but questioned how she was going to balance being a mother and a manager—a constant cry from women at the top of their tree.

She says that her clients and companies have been more than accommodating in this regard. In fact, she received major promotions and added responsibilities while pregnant with each child and made Managing Partner a year after her third son was born. She admits her career path is now somewhat smoother since her husband stays home and looks after the children so she can concentrate on her career.

DeHaas is certainly a disciplinarian when it comes to balancing home and work. She rises at 4:15 each morning to run 5 miles; she clearly states that this is *her time*. While on the treadmill, she plans her day and maintains it is a great stress reliever. If she does not have an evening commitment, she is home by early evening. Weekends are off-limits to work and strictly family time.

From the point of view of ambition and being female, DeHaas is certainly working for the right company. Deloitte launched the Women's Initiative in 1993 when some troubling data came to the attention of the CEO and Chairman, J. Michael Cook; only four out of fifty of the candidates for partner that year were women even though the firm had been hiring men and women in equal numbers since 1980. In addition, women were leaving at a significantly greater rate than men and not staying long enough to make it to partner.

In a profession defined by the competition for talent, this exodus was a business issue that could greatly affect the future of the firm. To find out why the firm was losing so many women, Cook established and chaired the Task Force for the Retention and Advancement of Women in 1992.

The yearlong research included meeting with corporations recognized as leaders in retaining and advancing women to identify best practices and determine results by conducting focus groups. Interviews were held with existing employees, to determine how they felt about working at Deloitte, together with interviewing forty of the high-potential women who had left the firm in recent years.

The results were startling—the majority of the women who had left were working elsewhere. Less than 10% stayed home to raise children and they planned to return to the workforce. Overall, the Task Force identified three areas of importance to address:

- Deloitte was a male-dominated environment, which perpetuated assumptions about women;
- There were perceived obstacles to advancement; and
- Both men and women expressed a need for help in achieving a better work/life fit.

Fourteen years later, Deloitte is a very different place—80% of employees say they would recommend Deloitte as a great place to work. Since 1997, Deloitte enjoys the highest percentage of women partners, principals, and directors among the Big Four professional services firms compared with those four women of the fifty newly admitted partners back in 1991. In summary, the Women's Initiative has helped Deloitte win new clients and new talent and has made the firm more successful in the marketplace. Thanks to the Women's Initiative, Deloitte was able to attract talented top leaders such as DeHaas.

DeHaas recognizes that the environment is constantly changing and she needs to be very responsive to that. Her goals for now are to make Deloitte a place where people feel good about working. Her clients already feel that they are served by high quality and committed people but DeHaas wants to take the business to the next level and relishes the challenge of having a role where she can make a difference.

There is no doubt that DeHaas regards herself as very fortunate in her chosen career and in her chosen company. When asked about obstacles, she struggles to think of any. With responsibility for over 5,000 people, she cites the *vastness* of the company being a challenge. In her view, her job is about helping other people be more effective in what they need to do to serve their clients. In leadership terms, it is about breaking down barriers, helping other people solve problems, and being very engaged in those types of things. It is about being a servant leader.

REFERENCES

Dess, G.G., and J.C. Picken. 2000. Changing roles: Leadership in the 21st century. *Organizational Dynamics*, Winter: 18–33.

Greenleaf, R.K. 1977. *Servant leadership: A journey into the nature of legitimate power and greatness.* New York: Paulist Press.

Kouzes, J.M., and B.Z. Posner. 2003. *The five practices of exemplary leadership.* San Francisco: Pfeiffer, A Wiley Imprint.

Schein, E. 1985. *Organizational culture and leadership.* San Francisco: Jossey-Bass.

Chapter 12

Mentoring and the Family Business: Sondra Healy

I feel good about myself, my workmates, and the products we're making. I feel terrific that there's a heritage, a tradition...a generational thing. Grandparents, fathers, sons, and daughters are using these products.

MENTORING RELATIONSHIPS FOR LEADERSHIP AND INFLUENCE

Mentoring has become a well-recognized avenue for developing employees in organizations, as more-experienced employees take their less-experienced colleagues under their wing. The term "mentor" originated from a character in Greek mythology, who was trusted to step in for Odysseus, a father who left his son's education in Mentor's hands when he went off to battle the Trojans (Wilson and Elman 1990). Mentoring includes offering "advice, information, or guidance by a person with useful experience, skills, or expertise for another individual's personal and professional development" (Luecke 2004, 76). The benefits of mentoring are great for both the mentor and the mentoree. The long-lasting relationships that develop may result in greater influence in the organization for both parties, along with a ready successor for the mentor, and increased understanding of organizational ethics, influence, and leadership on the part of the mentoree (Hughes, Ginnett, and Curphy 2006).

As Co-Chairman of Turtle Wax for the last thirty years, Sondra Healy leads possibly the best-known supplier of car care products in the world, and one with the majority of market share. She is proud to say that some of her employees have been with the company for more than thirty years and their children have continued the trend of being Turtle Wax employees. This loyalty to a family business is due in part to the family-like culture that Healy has created and maintained, along with the emphasis on mentoring those she employs.

Sondra Healy

FAMILY ROOTS AND MENTORING

Her father, Ben Hirsch, founded the company in the early 1940s with just $500. He operated a small storefront manufacturing facility on Clark Street in Chicago and had several different storefront locations over the years. In the early days, he made the product by hand in the bathtub with the help of his wife, Marie. From the start, Ben Hirsch had a major impact on her growing years. He encouraged her to always believe in herself and what she was doing and consequently Healy grew up loving work and working with people; this has been her driving force.

Healy seems to be a "natural-born" mentor (Luecke 2004, 100), strengthened no doubt by the personal development inspired by her father. *My father was my role model because he was so supportive and worked so hard, with honesty and integrity, and brought me along.* Healy fondly remembers her teenage years when she would wake up during the night to find the kitchen light on and her father working away. He would encourage her to sit with him, with her crackers and milk, and open her up to new ideas. "I don't care where an idea comes from," he would say, "just let's see what we can do with it."

There is no doubt that, as a young child having such an entrepreneurial father, Healy had a fascinating upbringing. She was born in St. Louis and attended a total of seven schools in Oklahoma and Chicago before graduating from high school. While she admits it was tough to constantly be introduced to new teachers and children, the idea of change never fazed her, and this early experience with it has helped creativity and innovation to flourish within Turtle Wax.

One of Healy's first loves was theater and she attended Lake Erie College in Ohio. She later received her BFA from the Goodman Theatre School of Drama in Chicago. She then lived in Los Angeles where she worked and performed in theatre. During this time, her father became ill and so she returned home to Chicago to study for her Masters in Education. She began teaching drama but her teaching career ended abruptly when her father passed away. Finding herself at a sudden crossroads, she took the time to reflect on what she planned to do next.

Healy's father had so inspired her with his beliefs in people, the faith he had in his products, and the importance of his business that her course of action seemed obvious—enter the family business. Her sense of wanting to preserve all that he had built was incredibly strong and so she stepped in to take up the reins. Only a few years later, she met her future husband, Denis Healy, at a trade show in Florida. Denis was the Director of Development for a consumer products company and they joined forces to build and retain the integrity of Turtle Wax. Denis had an entrepreneurial spirit (holding seven patents) and an amazing work ethic. They now serve as Chairmen of the company. Their son, Denis John, is CEO.

STEPPING INTO THE LEADERSHIP ROLE

It is clear that Healy is a people person and this must have been a tremendous asset in the early days. Recognizing that change is not always easy for employees, Healy was careful not to be presumptuous and decided to enter the company as Director of Public Relations, which is more of a generalist role. With her arts background, she loved interacting with the production and art departments, but quickly realized that she would have to integrate herself carefully into these areas. *You can't just jump into things especially if you value the people who were there.* In addition, she sat on advisory panels of manufacturing associations, dealing with such issues as the misuse of aerosols in Washington DC and started to network and get herself known in the automotive industry.

It is clear that, through the early years, Healy's principle motivating factor was how she valued her coworkers and the customers who had been loyal to her father's business. While the start of her career at Turtle Wax meant a steep learning curve in the early days, Healy counts herself lucky that she was able to overcome obstacles along the way. However, she notes that there are some challenges unique to a family business in the sense that sometimes hard decisions have to be made that impact other immediate family members. In addition, *when you work so closely in a family business everyone is regarded as family,* and at Turtle Wax, Healy is especially aware of the communication links between employees and her own family members. Her door was always open and consequently she soon gained the confidence of her employees and learned quickly from the ground floor up.

LEADING WITH VALUES

Healy is passionate about her family and personal beliefs, but with a cosmopolitan attitude. Her personal values are rooted in her Christian religion, and, with a family that included Episcopalians, Jews, Baptists, Catholics, and Protestants, she learned to value and love all religions. She believes that at the core people are *not to be judgmental in how you treat others;* this belief is at the core of everything Healy does.

She hopes that her employees feel the same way. The company's vision is grounded in ethics. *I'll give it to you verbatim...working together with our employees, creating the best products that we can with quality assurance in an ethical manner...how we present ourselves to our consumers and at large, and how we value our products threads through our entire organization.*

One of the keys to the culture that stems from Healy's values and vision is the expectation that everyone should treat their fellow coworkers with respect. Healy admits it doesn't always work that way and there have been occasions when employees have had to be let go because they didn't fit in. In these cases, her actions as a leader are congruent with her values, and that helps to maintain the strong family culture (Schein 1985). Healy has faced an ethical dilemma when dealing with an employee who did not fit in. *There are times some people are more exploitative, and they can be more belittling, not valuing some people. Either through an educational thing, or with a psychologist, people have to know that you are aware of the situation and are trying to correct it. Bring in counselors. They may not be aware that they are pressing buttons.*

From the beginning, Healy wanted open communication with her employees and that is still her mantra today. She very much values people's opinions and decisions and insists on an interchange of ideas throughout the company. Healy explains that you *have to have as much of an open dialogue as you can. Let them have their due; if you're having a meeting, this is their meeting.* One example of how Healy's leadership philosophy has paid off for Turtle Wax is when one of the large industrial unions approached the workers about forming a union within the company. After months of discussions, the employees decided against it, mainly because they decided that the communication links were so good within the company that they didn't need the union. This clearly meant a lot to her and she bursts with pride when telling the story!

FROM MENTOREE TO MENTOR

Since Healy knows every one of her employees so well and takes such a keen interest in them, mentoring comes naturally to her. Healy is justifiably proud about some of her employees' stories. Turtle Wax has ongoing training programs in different subjects including English, math, and computer science so that everyone has the opportunity to experience a better life. One of her Hispanic employees came up to her recently and glowingly told her that, thanks to these programs, his children have all received college educations and his daughter is now a lawyer. Stories like this just *warm me up* says Healy.

To her, the success of the business is as much about the excitement of working alongside people who share her same desire as it is about selling products. When traveling overseas, she constantly meets up with her distributors, some of whom have been working with Turtle Wax for fifty years. When they do eventually choose to retire, they still ask to come to work "for a couple of days a week"—such is the charisma of Turtle Wax.

She also quotes Winston Churchill as another role model—she especially likes Churchill's dogged approach regarding failure "When you fail—just continue and don't have less enthusiasm going forward." Healy certainly acts on these thoughts and relentlessly pursues new ideas in her constant push to keep the growth of Turtle Wax on a steady course. This aspect of her personality is invaluable when she gets involved in research and development projects at Turtle Wax—an aspect of the business she particularly enjoys. Being visionary and creative, she often suggests changes to new product designs as she has the ability to see products differently than others. She is, however, always mindful of the huge talent pool she has at Turtle Wax who really value seeing products brought to fruition and really enjoy what they are doing. It is probably one of the reasons why she has such a stable and loyal workforce of over 1,000 employees.

Healy also works hard at being a mentor outside the business. For some years, she has been involved in a mentoring program at Lady of Mercy School, starting with students as early as fourth grade. She initially thought it would be *just for a couple of years,* but was amazed to discover that the program extends right through to high school. Nonetheless, she has stuck with it and clearly thrives on trips to museums, fairs, and the seashore and loves acting as the *listening board* for students and being able to impact young people's lives.

Children and family mean everything to Healy, and it was a natural progression for her to get involved in JA's (Junior Achievement) business mentoring program, her husband Denis being an active member of JA. JA develops hands-on experiences to help young people understand the economics of life, and in partnership with business and educators, it brings the real world to students, opening their minds to their potential. JA offers programs in Economics, Project Business, and Business Basics, among others, and over two million students per year take part in their programs in nearly 100 nations and in 36 languages.

JA allows Healy to mix with different community leaders, including school principals, to work on mentoring programs involving interaction and teamwork and getting ideas across positively. Success to her is being able to get into the community and ripple the effect of teaching young people the lessons of learning how to make a better life for themselves and others. It is a great opportunity at meetings such as these for Healy to discuss her own role models and mentors, which, first and foremost, include her father. His pioneering attitude has stayed with Healy throughout her life.

AN INFLUENTIAL FUTURE

It is the flair for creativity that has brought Healy full circle back to her first love—the theater. She and her husband are producing a new musical, "Ancient City." It is a story of the effects of the UN decree creating the state of Israel. It chronicles the effects this decree had upon the lives of people living together for centuries, sharing their lives, endeavors, enterprises, and land, but having these things torn by outside forces.

In "Ancient City," the spirit of the land and the spiritual elements of the religions take hold and rivet the characters and audience toward a future life with a possibility of hope and peace.

All the ingredients in Healy's life—family, love, living peacefully in the community, caring and valuing others—comes out in the musical and it is clearly a cause dear to her heart. It is one of Healy's biggest accomplishments so far and she is hoping to take the musical overseas to reach a wider audience. In her eyes, you can elevate people's consciences through the arts and it is another way to capture the attention of young people.

There is no question that Healy has power but it is a word that she dislikes. To her, it is far more important to be regarded as successful and to have a positive approach, because that is what permeates through to everyone in the company. With 1,000 people working at Turtle Wax, she has a tough leadership assignment, but Healy is keen to grow the business even more. That way, she can help even more people and have an even greater impact mentoring employees to do the best they can.

REFERENCES

Hughes, R.L., R.C. Ginnett, and G.J. Curphy. 2006. *Leadership: Enhancing the lessons of experience*. 5th ed. New York: McGraw-Hill/Irwin.

Luecke, R. 2004. *Coaching and mentoring: How to develop top talent and achieve stronger performance*. Boston: Harvard Business School Publishing Corporation.

Schein, E. 1985. *Organizational culture and leadership*. San Francisco: Jossey-Bass.

Wilson, J.A., and N.S. Elman. 1990. Organizational benefits of mentoring. *Academy of Management Executive* 4: 88–93.

Chapter 13

Social Commitment and Entrepreneurship: Dr. Mary Ann Leeper

For me it's always about what we are doing. It isn't about me as a person. It's about what we are trying to accomplish—bringing the female condom to women in the developing world who desperately want and need it.

Social entrepreneurship—with its unofficial motto, "doing good while doing well"—marries the economic tools of capitalism with social goals. Those who work in this hybrid arena measure their success by more than just a financial bottom line. While rising interest in corporate social responsibility has even conventional businesses talking in terms of "triple bottom lines," social and environmental goals are still subordinate to financial performance. In contrast, social entrepreneurs go further, making their social, humanitarian, or environmental mission at least as important as their financial goals, and in some instances, the primary mission.

Such has been the case for Dr. Mary Ann Leeper, President and COO of the Female Health Company. A biochemist who had risen through the management ranks of several pharmaceutical companies, Leeper left corporate life in the mid-1980s to start up an investment development company focusing on finding small manufacturing and marketing companies in the pharmaceutical, specialty chemicals, and/or branded consumer products areas. In the search for investment opportunities, Leeper met a Danish physician, Lasse Hessel, who had invented a prototype condom for women to use. Leeper became intensely interested in the new product—the female condom. At the time, developing this product for the North American market seemed like a surefire commercial opportunity. Even later when Leeper's company reorganized and created a new company around this single product, she knew her business had strong social goals but she could not have imagined that she would become a social entrepreneur focused only on the mission of accessibility of the female condom. Years later,

Dr. Mary Ann Leeper

powered by her mission to enable women worldwide to protect themselves against HIV/AIDS, the constantly evolving experience of social entrepreneurship with its discovery, struggle, and improvisation still fascinates her.

BRINGING NEW PRODUCTS TO THE DEVELOPING WORLD THROUGH STRATEGIC GLOBAL ALLIANCES

Based in a small corporate office in Chicago, the for-profit, publicly traded Female Health Company (OTC: FHCO) owns patents and exclusive worldwide rights to manufacture, market, and sell the female condom, which is the first and only female-initiated barrier method for contraception and disease prevention. The device, now manufactured at a facility in the UK, is made of a sheer, non-latex, polyurethane material, shaped like a sheath with flexible O rings on each end. One ring inside the sheath is used to insert the device, somewhat like a diaphragm over the cervix, while the other ring formed an opening outside of the vagina. Leeper ushered the device through a long FDA approval process, demonstrating that the female condom is as, if not more, effective as the male condom in preventing unintended pregnancy and STDs. As important, however, a woman could control its use and did not have to rely on her partner to use a male condom.

Today, the female condom is sold commercially in ten countries and distributed by public sector agencies in more than ninety countries, including the developing world.

Given the personal nature of her company's product and the complexity of her business, Leeper finds it simplest to say, *I just work for a small women's health company* when introducing herself to someone in passing. *But,* she adds,

> *If they are genuinely interested, I explain that I work for the Female Health Company, we make the FC female condom®, and we do most of our work in the developing world. For me it's always about what we are doing. It isn't about me as a person. It's about what we're trying to accomplish—bringing the female condom to women in the developing world.*

Although Leeper downplays her influence, it has been her perceptive, adaptive, and intrepid leadership that has fueled the company's growth and made her a leading authority on international public health issues, particularly in the developing world. Perhaps her greatest achievement has been the vast set of relationships she has created around the world *to bring the female condom to "the woman on the street, in her village, where she lives"* as she puts it. The list of entities with which Leeper has negotiated and created alliances is legion, including the World Health Organization, the Joint United Nations Global Programme on HIV/AIDS, the U.S. Agency for International Development, International Planned Parenthood Federation, Family Health International, Population Services International, ministries of public health in numerous countries throughout the world, particularly in developing countries, not to mention the FDA and many U.S. city and state public health agencies.

LEARNING THROUGH OBSERVATION FROM EARLY ROLE MODELS

What accounts for Leeper's unusually perceptive leadership? For this answer, we might go back to Drexel Hill, PA, a suburb of Philadelphia.

> *I grew up in a household of women—my mother, two sisters and two aunts—there was no male influence really at all. Personal issues fall out from that kind of environment, so I'm very sensitive to women. And I think that is how I learned to be observant. The only way I learned behavior and practice was observing, because my mother was always working. No one around to teach you. My values come from her, no question, but learning to observe, clearly, that's how I did it.*

Indeed, Leeper counts her mother as a role model, along with Eleanor Roosevelt and Katherine Hepburn. But Leeper credits her eighth grade teacher, Sister Rita Bernadette, for *taking me outside of myself. Until then I was always in the back observing.*

I developed a trust with her that I didn't have with anyone. My father died when I was ten, so I kind of went into a shell. But she encouraged me to have more self-confidence. She told me I was very bright. You know they used to do IQ tests, and I was pretty high, so I remember her telling me that. She taught me to think outside the box. We talked about science. In those days we had the same teacher all day long for all subjects. Interesting, my eighth grade class had a 50th reunion this summer. I couldn't go, but I sent an e-mail to the list, and Tony Gucci wrote to me and he said, you and I were really good friends with Sister Rita Bernadette, weren't we? He was always getting into trouble.

Sister Rita Bernadette's influence can be seen easily in Leeper's academic accomplishments. Leeper earned a Ph.D. in pharmaceutical chemistry from Temple University and later completed an MBA at Northwestern University's Kellogg School of Management. Despite these advanced degrees, Leeper only counts her education as a limited part of her development as a leader: *Leadership isn't just learned from attending a class, but attending the class is additive to reading, listening, observing, integrating. You can't learn anything I did in a book.* Interestingly enough, Leeper's self-assessment comes very close to a characteristic that Bennis and Thomas identify, in a phrase borrowed from Saul Bellow, as a less obvious asset of leaders: "[T]hey are 'first-class noticers.' Being a first-class noticer allows you to recognize talent, identify opportunities, and avoid pitfalls. Leaders who succeed again and again are geniuses at grasping context" (Bennis and Thomas 2002, 19).

Throughout the time she has developed the female condom and her company, Leeper has relied on her skill as a "first-class noticer" and combined it with an amazingly resourceful ability to adapt. As she reports, *My motivation is to get the job done—to bring the female condom to women who need it and to make the Female Health Company successful. I'm not an inventor, but I say, "Here's something that is interesting, and how does that help me do what I need to do?"*

THE EMERGENCE OF A SOCIAL ENTREPRENEUR

Necessity and Leeper's commitment to getting the job done, while remaining flexible about how to do it, are what eventually led her to evolve into a social entrepreneur. When Leeper first brought the female condom to market, she and others she worked with viewed the challenge as a fairly straightforward new product development project—see the product through the FDA, brand and market it using conventional methods, position it as the alternative to existing products, in this case the male condom. In 1993, after prolonged FDA clinical trials, the female condom began limited distribution in the United States. Under the trademark "Reality" and with the tagline "Count on Yourself," the female condom was promoted to empower women to protect themselves against STD and HIV infection. The product was sold in drugstores, but was also available through public health clinics. But even with a huge advertising push, the commercial market responded poorly.

Despite the hefty cost, the whole campaign flopped. Within six weeks of the national launch, I knew we were in for a struggle. Most of the typically white, young, college women we were trying to reach simply did not hear the message. Intellectually they thought it was a good idea to be able to protect themselves, but emotionally, in the heat of the moment, forget it—safe sex stayed outside the bedroom! These young women really did not recognize they were at risk of getting an STD, let alone the possibility of being infected with HIV and dying from sex. As an added bonus to our dilemma, the media jeered at the female condom. Numerous jokes and embarrassed laughter littered the pages of women's magazines. Something had to be done.

In spite of her frustration, Leeper turned to the sources that she knew mattered the most—the people who were actually interested in and using the product. Through conversations with employees who answered the consumer information line and listening into calls herself, Leeper's picture of Reality's target market began to change. Inquiries and calls were coming from all kinds of women—and men!—not just young, white affluent women. Many mentioned that they had heard about the product from a friend. A larger than expected portion of the responses came from women of color. Some of the women and men were in long-standing relationships or married. Often the questions asked were not about the product, so much as how to suggest using the female condom to a person's partner. But the overwhelming commonality was that the people most open to using the product truly believed that they were at risk.

As a result of what she was hearing—*This information hit me like a lightning bolt*—Leeper began adapting. Eventually, product promotions were modified to take into account the unique needs of female condom users. To appeal more to people in relationships than to the image of a one-night stand, print ads showed a romantic couple looking into each other's eyes with a new tagline, "Feels so good, you won't believe it's safer sex."

Leeper's attention was drawn increasingly toward the public sector. She began to understand that she not only had a product to sell, but in order for the product to be used, several other steps had to already be in place. A potential user had to believe she was truly at risk so she would be motivated to protect herself, she needed to learn about the product from a trusted and knowledgeable source, and she needed help introducing the alternative method to her partner. Seeing the "sale" in context, Leeper developed a program that shifted from a one-way product promotion to two-way dialogue about a very sensitive and personal health concern. Instead of focusing narrowly on making a transaction which was consistent with a commercial model, Leeper had to refocus on enabling healthful conversations in a holistic network of relationships, which was more consistent with a public health model.

As Richard Perloff writes, "[T]he story of AIDS is...a uniquely human story—one that fundamentally requires us to apply the powers of the mind to help master irrational fears, seemingly uncontrollable emotions, and sexual habits of the heart" (Perloff 2001, vii). Such problems came up for Leeper and her company. For example, many potential users were in denial about how high their risk of contracting HIV actually was. Doctors and clinic workers needed to be encouraged to recommend the product and help users overcome initial apprehensions. Women needed coaching and role playing to learn the assertiveness skills necessary to negotiate the product into the context of her sexual relationship. As Leeper recalled

> *I had to develop a whole new communication program—a step-by-step program. The public sector campaign amounted to a "train the trainers" program designed to teach the counselors so they, in turn, could help their clients. This approach seemed to generate acceptance and satisfied users.*

Without completely meaning to, but out of necessity, Leeper had to become a health communication specialist, a role more commonly associated with public health agencies than profit-oriented businesses.

And then, out of no where, Leeper received a call from Daisy Nyamukapa, manager of the HIV/AIDS Coordination Programme for Zimbabwe's Ministry of Health and Child Welfare. This call changed the whole direction of the company and provided Leeper an opportunity to once again test her ability to adapt. Nyamukapa said she had a petition signed by 30,000 Zimbabwean women demanding that the government bring the female condom to their country. Women and children overwhelmingly represented most of the nearly three million with HIV/AIDS. Teenage girls suffered five to six times the infection rate of boys, and in one town 70% of women attending prenatal clinics were found infected. Zimbabwe was not alone; the impact of the disease was especially harsh in sub-Saharan Africa, and the disease was spreading in Asia and Latin America. With this phone call, Leeper's attention was drawn to the plight of women around the world who were threatened by HIV/AIDS and international efforts to combat the disease.

The challenges ahead increased exponentially as Leeper now needed to adjust not only to unique cultural and social conditions in each country but to the intricacies and politics of world health. On top of what she had learned about promoting the female condom and creating a communication program around it for the U.S. market, Leeper started to forge alliances around the world to enable her product to get into the hands of women who were desperate for it. She had to learn who the key players were, what were the cultural impacts to a "step-by-step" program for women in sub-Saharan Africa, and how to get the product to her "sisters" when it seemed that no one had any money to pay for it, including the Female Health Company. First, she negotiated an agreement with the UNAIDS (Joint United Nations Programme on HIV/AIDS) and the WHO (World Health Organization). The agreement formally endorsed the female condom as a tool to combat the spread of HIV, and 10,000 letters were sent to ministers of health in 152 developing nations. Although UNAIDS and WHO's blessing was essential politically, there was little initial response. Leeper soon discovered that she needed to establish lines of communication that did not yet exist between network organizations in order to distribute the female condom. Especially absent were communication lines between donor and aid organizations. At local levels, extensive efforts were needed to coordinate between many stakeholders, including political leaders, government institutions, local villagers, and even national soccer teams.

By listening and improvising, Leeper's objective became reframed and in so doing she became a social entrepreneur. The real "competition" was not the male condom but the practice of unsafe sex. The new objective had to be increasing the number of protected sexual encounters, with using the female condom becoming the means to that end rather than an end in itself. The campaign became *the program, not just the product.* But even more curious to the competitive sensibility of a for-profit company, Leeper advocates protection, regardless of whether achieved by using the female or the male condom, over advocating for the female condom alone. To Gregory Dees, this is the mark of the social entrepreneur: "[T]he social mission is explicit and central....Mission-related impact becomes the central criterion, not wealth creation. Wealth is just a means to an end for social entrepreneurs" (Dees 1998/2001, 2–3). Clarifying this end-means relationship is not only philosophical but practical. Leeper has learned that she could gain more through cooperation and building alliances. For example, especially in the public health sector and the developing world, the female condom piggybacks on distribution networks already well-established by the promotion of male condoms. In this context, it made more sense to offer the female condom as an alternative rather than a competition.

INFLUENCING SOCIAL CHANGE: THE FEMALE HEALTH FOUNDATION

Responding to the need to not only promote the female condom but influence the context in which it is introduced, adopted, and used, Leeper created the Female Health Foundation in 1996 as a not-for-profit sister organization supported by the Female Health Company. The relationship is symbiotic—what is good for one is good for the other—and structurally, the two entities work in tandem and form the organizational basis for Leeper's social entrepreneurship. The mission of the foundation is to support worldwide information, education, communication, and outreach programs that empower women and increase their well-being, particularly with regard to family planning and AIDS prevention. Strategically, the foundation focuses on the complex conditions under which the female condom will or will not be used. As the foundation Web site explains,

As the global leader in the field of female-initiated prevention technologies, the Female Health Foundation plays an important role in defining and articulating women's protection strategies. In so doing, we recognize

that gender power inequities shape women's ability to make and implement reproductive health choices, and their economic vulnerability fuels their sexual vulnerability. Moreover, we believe that the unequal status of girls and women in many societies is central to any discussion of protection strategies, and that the underlying task of changing the power balance between men and women is essential for real and sustained change.

MEETING ADVERSITY WITH PERSISTENCE AND CONVICTION

Almost paradoxically, the more Leeper has learned and adapted in the context of the world in which the female condom might be used, the stronger has grown her intrepid inner conviction. One after another, Leeper has overcome obstacles using her spunk, gumption, and ingenuity, while deepening her commitment to fight against HIV/AIDS. For example, despite his initial refusal, Leeper persuaded Hessel, the female condom's inventor, to work with her. When the female condom was reclassified as a Class III medical device in the middle of the FDA process, setting Leeper's progress back several years, she still prevailed. As new circumstances arose, Leeper met each set, acted, learned, integrated, and moved on to the next challenge.

This is not to say, however, that there have not been some very discouraging times. After the initial U.S. launch of the female condom floundered, Leeper's company went through a very major reorganization. Leeper's dexterity and faith have been tested significantly by the realities of being a publicly traded, for-profit company. Given the expense of FDA clinical trials and approval, not to mention the significant start up costs, organizing as a privately held company was untenable. The need for capital for a company like the Female Health Company virtually requires the pooled economic power of many shareholders. As such, on many occasions, Leeper has had to cajole her board and investors by reminding them that theirs is an investment for the very long haul. The financial picture while continuing to be a roller coaster looks bright. In 2003, the Female Health Company broke even for the first time. But in 2004 Leeper lost an order for four million units due to a scandal in Brazil. To which she says *That's the world that I work in. You go along banging your head against the wall and then things turn around, the sun comes out and the held-up order finally comes through.* In 2006, the company saw another upturn when it posted a positive net income. Leeper reports that major countries' ministries of health, as well as global public health agencies, are giving strong continued support for increasing purchases of the FC female condom and for its crucial program implementation.

While usually more than up to the task, the enormity of the struggle with the business and to achieve her mission has at times taken their toll on Leeper. A particularly low point came one Easter Sunday. Leeper was working in her office, sitting at a long conference table covered with documents.

After several years and millions of dollars, the Female Health Company and Leeper were on the brink.

> *I was ready to give up out of total frustration. At that time in my career, I had all the experience of corporate learning. I don't think I could have started everything I did in the late 80s if I had not gone through all the training and mentoring that I got in the corporate world. I was just beginning to put the pieces together. But at that moment, I thought "What have I done? I'm at my wit's end." It wasn't worth it, because I don't do things for financial goals, that's obvious, but I wasn't getting anything back intrinsically. All I kept getting back was negative, negative frustration. It is very debilitating to me when I get that over and over again.*

Just then the phone rang. The woman on the other end apologized for calling on Easter, but she had heard Leeper worked a lot and she wanted to call "while he's not here." As they talked, Leeper learned that she was speaking to Anna, a woman from Harlem. Anna's partner was HIV positive and had beaten her in the past when she asked him to use a (male) condom. Since Anna was financially dependent on him, she felt leaving was not an option. Recently, however, Anna had been using the female condom without her partner noticing.

> *She called and said what you are doing is really important and it is helping me and my sisters. That changed my whole perspective. It was an absolutely pivotal moment in my life.*

Leeper also describes that moment as "transformational." In a moment of truth with a woman she was desperate to help, Leeper's faith in her mission was resurrected. Anna's call was almost mystical. When asked what she would have done if Anna had not called, Leeper simply says, *I don't know. I haven't a clue.*

REPLENISHING THE WELL: A TIME FOR REFLECTION AND REINVENTION

The need for renewal faces any leader from time to time. Leeper rejects trite solutions, such as sleeping in or going fishing for a weekend.

> *The essence of who you are is weary and bored and whatever. So taking a weekend off with your husband or sleeping 24 hours a day is not going to regenerate that....Ultimately, I say, "This path that you are on—let's figure out a new path, strategy, direction." I make the decision I have to do something and something will trigger a new way.*

These days Leeper contemplates retiring and grooming a successor, and she jokes that she hopes she doesn't have another idea, which seems very unlikely. In fact, she has just begun a new project called the BWI (Business Women's Initiative) against HIV/AIDS, an organization that she has cofounded with Mary Robinson, former UN High Commissioner for Human Rights and former President of Ireland. Leeper got the idea for the initiative after being prompted by a session at the 2004 World AIDS Conference to think about how she could bring business women and their skills into the fight against HIV/AIDS.

This opportunity with BWI, to encourage business women to look at their sisters in the developing world and apply their skills, looking at problems from their perspectives and coming up with answers is very energizing to me. I'm so glad to get Mary Robinson involved—the impact could be not just on the female condom, but more importantly on those women. It could be amazingly wonderful, even if it is just one little piece it will be fantastic. So this piece has reenergized me so I can say, okay, I'm not going to retire yet.

REFERENCES

Bennis, Warren G., and Robert J. Thomas. 2002. *Geeks & geezers: How era, values, and defining moments shape leaders.* Boston: Harvard Business School Press.

Dees, J. Gregory. 1998. Revised 2001. The meaning of "social entrepreneurship." Center for Advancement of Social Entrepreneurship, Duke University, http://www.fuqua.duke.edu/centers/case/documents/dees_sedef.pdf (accessed March 10, 2007).

Perloff, Richard M. 2001. *Persuading people to have safer sex: Applications of social science to the AIDS crisis.* Mahwah, NJ: Lawrence Erlbaum Associates.

Chapter 14

The Power of Confidence with Being in Charge: Madeleine W. Ludlow

I like being the boss.

Having worked her way up in finance and learned C-suite level leadership lessons, Madeleine Ludlow has just started her own Cincinnati-based investment banking firm, targeting middle market private companies.

It's really come together this week. We raised capital for our own firm...and just this week I think we're at 90 percent of the money we need. Today or Monday we will have our first client. I don't even have office space! I can't tell you how excited I am.

THE POWER OF "INFLUENCE"

At root, two fundamentals have helped Ludlow progress to this point in her career: she likes being in charge, and she has the self-confidence to do it.

Like many women, Ludlow says she is not sure she would label this as seeking out "power" per se. A look at Ludlow's life, however, shows that her upbringing, schooling, and work experiences prepared her well to become a competent, assertive leader focused not so much on having control and status, but on making a difference. The ambivalence many women have about the word "power" is understandable given the all too easy stereotypes of women using power as manipulation, guile, or helplessness. Some women say they feel more comfortable with the term "influence" and contrast having influence with having status. Articles in publications such as *Fast Company* and *Fortune* reveal that women leaders themselves have yet to reach consensus on differences and similarities between men and women's leadership styles (Muoio 1998; Sellers 2003). CEO of Benchmark Communications,

Madeleine W. Ludlow

Judith Glaser, writes that "power and leadership are being redefined. No longer are we comfortable equating leadership with force and power with dominance" (Glaser 2006). In their study of women political leaders, psychologists Dorothy Cantor and Toni Bernay write that the essential equation of women's leadership equals the sum of a competent self and creative forcefulness, applied to making other people's lives better (Cantor and Bernay 1992). Very much, they say, a woman's leadership ability emerges as a function of her self-confidence, and Ludlow's example appears to support this insight well.

THE EARLY EMERGENCE OF SELF-CONFIDENCE

Ludlow says she had a privileged childhood and credits her father with setting high expectations for what she could become.

> *I never remember a day in my entire life that I didn't think that I was going to graduate school. I can't say I remember the specific day when he said what he said. It was always expected that I would do well in school and go to college and then go on to graduate school, maybe because I was the oldest. My brother did the same thing, but my sisters haven't.*

Attending Emma Willard, a private girls' school in upstate New York, also shaped her future leadership style.

> *My dad said you can go to the best place you want to go. Those teachers believed in girls. Emma Willard, who founded the school, was the first woman*

to teach girls science and math in an institutional setting. They just believed that girls could do whatever they wanted.

In this context, Ludlow never learned to distrust herself the way some girls do in high school, particularly with regard to math and science. While Ludlow primarily thinks of the confidence she gained as an asset, there have been times when she has been surprised that she couldn't take for granted that other people could handle it. When doing some pro bono work for the school, Ludlow told the head master

> *Emma Willard is part of my problem. You taught us to speak our mind, and you also taught us that people would actually care about what we had to say. I've lived my life that way, and there are certainly situations where people have cared and others where even though they said they wanted to, they didn't.*

After graduating in 1978 with an MBA from the Darden Graduate Business School at the University of Virginia, Ludlow worked at firms including Bank of America, Morgan Stanley, and Public Service Electric and Gas in Newark, NJ. Ludlow recalled, *When I got to Morgan Stanley, there were practically no women. There were only two women in the firm who were more senior than me.* Ludlow credits the Emma Willard school for the confidence she had in the nearly all-male setting: *I have more self-confidence than any human ought to have. I think I walked into environments that were primarily male and assumed it didn't matter.* Ludlow's confidence paid off: *I was making tons of money; I'd never made so much.*

At the same time, the pace was grueling. Ludlow and her husband tried for years to have a baby until Ben was born in 1989.

> *When I came back from having Ben, they were shocked. I came back to work, which meant I would be living the lifestyle. The year after Ben was born I was working 70 hours a week and commuting an hour and a half each way. Most women just didn't come back to work. I was one of only a handful of women to have a child and stay on at Morgan Stanley. So I went to my boss and said I would really like to work four days a week. He could cut my pay, and I'd work at home on Fridays. He said "we don't have part-time employees," so I left.*

EXPLORING A NEW PATH

Ludlow went to work for small investment banking firms, thinking that they might help her *find a balance between having a baby and a life,* but she said, *in the end they were worse....With a small firm, you make no money. If there's a lot of business you don't have the resources that we had at Morgan Stanley, so I said this isn't working.*

Luckily, Bob Murray—*the best boss I ever had*—got in touch with Ludlow around that time. Murray had been a partner at Morgan Stanley and was one of Ludlow's mentors: *He was definitely a mentor, someone who was there for me in much more of a way than a boss would have been. Murray had gone to Public Services and was looking for a treasurer for their largest subsidiary. He asked me if I wanted to do it, and I said yes.*

In 1997 Ludlow became CFO of Cinergy, a Cincinnati-based energy company. Having excelled in the technical dimensions of finance, Ludlow now needed to learn the arts of management and diplomacy. In general, Ludlow thought that finance was a good field for women because it was more measurable. In other words, she could demonstrate quantitatively her value to the organization. For Ludlow, the CFO position was a natural fit because she could apply the multitasking skills she had learned as a working mother: *When you're the CFO of a company you have to deal with 10 different issues all the time.*

At the same time, Ludlow confesses that she had a lot to learn.

> *When I came to Cinergy, I'd never been in a senior management position. I'd had a fair amount of responsibility before, but never managed people much except within my own group. The CEO of Cinergy loved what he saw in me and thought I had all the skills I needed. But what I didn't have in 1997 was someone who would sit me down and say, "this is how you deal with a senior management team." I was very poor at the politics. I tend to take things at face value, but you can't assume that everyone is seeing the world the way you see it.*

Ludlow thinks her biggest mistakes were caused by making some of her arguments publicly in meetings when they would probably have been better received in one-on-one conversations. *Sometimes those are good conversations to have, but there's also a time when you shut up and go in separately to your boss and have that conversation one-on-one. It took me about a year and a half to figure out what I was doing and by then I'd set the stage.... You've got to admit you're still learning.*

Next, in 2000, Ludlow became CEO of Cadence Network, an Internet-based service company in which Cinergy was an investor. Cadence offered professional services and software applications designed to help companies with many departments, vendors, and geographically dispersed locations manage utility expenses, such as electric, gas, telecommunications, water, sewer, lease, and waste management. At the height of the dot-com craze, Cadence's venture capitalist investors lured Ludlow with grand plans of making millions and taking the company public. As with many dot-coms, reality didn't quite live up to the dreams, although in contrast to the many companies that went under, Ludlow's tough leadership saved the company.

When Ludlow arrived, Cadence was losing $1.5 million a month, so the only solution to *stop the bleeding* was to let people go.

> *It's the hardest thing I ever did. We let 20 people go at a time. I was running the company, so ultimately I had to make these choices. It was really important*

to me that everybody understood why and that we treated everyone with respect when we did it. As much as we could, we helped them emotionally and financially. I never wanted to treat them that way....[By] the year after I got there we had taken the company from 105 to 35 people. We had no money. We were on life support. I spent the next two years after that getting the company to a point where it could survive. And it is now surviving, but there's no growth in it. I didn't leave the job I had [at Cinergy] to go run a tiny little company that wasn't going anywhere.

So in January 2004, Ludlow handed the CEO title to the President and COO, but she has stayed on as chairman of the board. Initially, Ludlow was on an eight-month consulting contract, but when senior management at Cadence never called for advice, those eight months became something of a sabbatical, time to spend with her husband and son. *So I essentially took 2004 off and stayed home. I had never been home with my son since he was born, and it was a fabulous experience to be home when he was 15.*

ON INTEGRITY AND MAKING A DIFFERENCE

Of all her personal values, Ludlow prides herself most on her integrity and giving back. *I just can't tell a lie,* she explains, *that's how you can control your own integrity.* Ludlow's belief in integrity has run like a theme throughout her life: *My dad was that kind of person, U.Va. had an honor code, and Morgan Stanley is that kind of place, honest and ethical.* As for giving back, Ludlow has done her own share of mentoring and does her best to be involved in her community. She counts herself among those who are overcommitted yet effective: *You give a busy person one more thing to do, and they get it done.* Ludlow gives her time and money generously, but is quick to add, *I feel very strongly that we should all make a difference, but I have to be careful that I don't get so wrapped up in that that I forget to come home for dinner!* Ludlow's church is especially important to her, calling it *a real comfort. It makes such a difference on a Sunday morning.*

THE PASSION FOR ENTREPRENEURSHIP: BEING THE DECISION-MAKER

These days Ludlow looks forward to being her own boss. *I really like being the boss. When I was at Cadence, I was the boss so I got to decide what kind of culture we had there. I believe the culture of a company comes from the very top, so ours was a culture of being kind to people, being open, a culture of ethical dealings with people. I loved the fact that I could decide that that was the way we were going to deal with people.* For now Ludlow looks forward to establishing her new business. When asked what she imagines is the ideal organization, she quips, *The ideal organization has two people, and you are one of the partners! I've never been more excited.*

REFERENCES

Cantor, Dorothy W., and Toni Bernay with Jean Stoess. 1992. *Women in power: The secrets of leadership.* Boston: Houghton Mifflin.
Glaser, Judith E. 2006. Power and influence: Decipher the language of leadership. *Leadership Excellence* 16.
Muoio, Anna. 1998. Women and men, work and power. *Fast Company,* no. 13:71.
Sellers, Patricia. 2003. Power: Do women really want it? *Fortune* 148 (8): 80–100.

Chapter 15

Creativity as a Source for Leadership: Eva Maddox

*Good design addresses problems, promotes business in an ethical climate, creates
productive work environments and is not mere decoration. . . .
Design shapes the way we live. So it ought to serve everyone.*

Artistic creativity is a rare and desirable talent or trait. Yet seldom is creative talent associated with leadership. Eva Maddox is a notable exception. From her modest beginnings in a small town in middle Tennessee, she has become one of the top commercial designers in the United States today. As founder and president of EMA (Eva Maddox Associates), she provided leadership, motivation, design direction, and overall vision for her firm while working with clients such as DuPont, Tootsie Roll, Hallmark, Bank of America, and Ogilvy & Mather. Her logo, "Branded Environments," reflects a well-developed and evolving design philosophy that *embodies the idea that anyone who is connected with a company ought to be able to understand what the company does, what are its mission and values, and how it understands itself and its role in commerce or the community.* Cofounding Archeworks with Stanley Tigerman, a well-known architect in his own right, reflects her commitment to develop, train, and mentor future designers with the branded environments philosophy as their mission and mantra.

Maddox attributes much of her success to good luck. But luck does not account for her determination, hard work, assiduous networking, and relentless focus on her vision and goals, all elements that have resulted in extraordinary success. What is most interesting, however, is not luck or hard work, but rather how she has developed her idea of branded environments into a leadership story that integrates her personal values, creativity, and commitment to design and environmental sustainability with the ongoing evolution of a successful brand and business model. As a result, she is and lives Branded Environments in every way.

Eva Maddox

THE BIRTH OF A CREATIVE DESIGNER: EARLY INFLUENCES AND INTERESTS

According to Howard Gardner, "[l]eaders achieve their effectiveness chiefly through the stories they [embody] and relate....The ultimate impact of the leader depends most significantly on the particular story that he or she relates or embodies, and the receptions to that story on the part of audiences (or collaborators or followers)" (Gardner 1995, 9, 14). Effective and visionary leadership, according to Gardner, entails developing one's story and being able to communicate that story in ways that are both receptive and mind-altering. As a result, when the story is effective, both the leader and her collaborators develop a new vision that then becomes accepted as a standard. Eva Maddox's development of her creative design processes emulates such leadership development. How did this evolve?

Early on, Maddox had a keen interest in design and began her learning in a cooperative program in the College of Design, Architecture, Art, and Planning at the University of Cincinnati. In this program, students worked on different projects and jobs every other quarter, and studied the alternate quarters. Maddox graduated with a Bachelor of Science in design in the 1960s. In 2006, in recognition of her achievements, she received an honorary doctorate from that university.

After graduation, for the next few years Maddox worked in design in Cincinnati with Space Design while her husband, Lynn, was in graduate school. She traveled the state of Indiana looking for design opportunities and her firm let her create interior designs for any customers she was able to find. By the time she moved to Chicago in the early seventies, Maddox had close to ten years' experience of virtually knocking on doors and selling people on design. Before long, she was hired by a large firm in Chicago—RM&M (Richmond, Manhoff & Marsh)—one of the front-runners in corporate interiors at the time.

Maddox quickly realized that she wanted to concentrate on commercial design and worked with RM&M for a year. During that period she began thinking about design not merely as space or decoration but as a reflection of the person or company for whom the design was created. This meant that interior design was not something separate from the architecture in which it functioned. Maddox longed to reconnect her work with an architectural firm in order to coordinate interior design with architectural structure, and during the next year she joined Meister & Volpe, a partnership run by two architects. There she started an interiors group while meeting and networking with people in and around Chicago and getting herself well known in the corporate world for commercial design.

Maddox continued to look for new opportunities to expand her creative instincts by cooperating with other architects. She quotes one example of asking a colleague to introduce her to an important architect at a networking event. The colleague was reluctant, since the person was the well-known architect, Stanley Tigerman. But, true to her style, Maddox introduced herself, and Tigerman—her target—has been a good friend and mentor ever since. She cites Tigerman as being one of the people who really pushed her to do better work and to stretch herself, and in 1994 they cofounded Archeworks.

Soon it became clear to Maddox that she was bringing in more business than the others at Meister & Volpe, so she decided to start her own business. In 1975 she formed EMA. Maybe some luck came into play here as Maddox already had three large clients who followed her to EMA and who became critical for the development of her business. One was Larry Levy of the Levy Organization. A developer, he had noticed Maddox's talent early on and promised his support. Another great supporter was Irwin Steinberg, president of Mercury Records (now Polygram). Within four days of starting her own business, Irwin commissioned her to renovate his New York headquarters. The third client was the Options Clearing Corporation in Chicago. These three companies helped establish Maddox in the world of commercial design and put her firm, Eva Maddox Associates, "on the map."

THE IMPORTANCE OF SOCIAL CAPITAL

In those first days of the new firm, Maddox built a strong network of people which proved useful in building up the business over the next twenty-five years. She has remained in touch and in strong relationships with colleagues in the companies she left and with all her former and present clients. She would argue that networking is absolutely essential for developing a long-term and successful business model, and "burning one's bridges" is usually detrimental even when those with whom one is dealing are wrongheaded.

As part of networking, mentoring has played an important part in Maddox's career and she has always looked to people around her as role models. It is essential to have a mentor whom one can trust but who is both encouraging and critical. Her mother was her first role model—a woman who worked all her professional life as a high school counselor for the State of Tennessee. From an early age, Maddox always saw her mother as a professional, and it was only much later that she realized that during her childhood most women did not work and seldom thought of themselves in professional roles.

THE PASSION FOR BRAND IDENTITY

One of Maddox's early ideas in the 1970s was in the arena of brand identification, and she acknowledges that much of what she is doing now ties back to that period. Most architects and designers in the 1970s and 1980s were engrossed in designing only the façade of a building, or in presenting interior ornamentation and decoration that did not necessarily coordinate with the architecture, theme, and mission of the organization for whom this work was designed. Maddox became passionate about working with clients to develop their brand identity and a unique message—something very innovative in commercial design. At the same time while building her story around branded environments, she was also changing the mind-sets of clients and eventually of designers. Thus, both her creativity and her strong client base enabled Maddox to change the philosophy of design from decoration to a more holistic approach.

Corporate design in the mid-1970s was enjoying a real boom and remained her focus for several years. Always on the lookout for the next opportunity, though, EMA moved into showroom, exhibit, and retail work. Her company soon became highly valued for its innovative design ideas and being among the first to invent new ways to link design with the philosophy and identity of the organization. As a result, her company won many prestigious awards and Maddox herself became recognized as one of the great innovators of her generation.

EMA also became well-known for producing measurable financial results for its clients. The Branded Environments approach to strategic planning and design solutions was pioneered by EMA in the mid-1980s. The philosophy behind the approach is to define the strategic essence of an institution, its products, or service identity (brand), and then to integrate that essence into the physical surroundings, through the products or service the client delivers, and into the mind-sets of its employees and professionals. Design today, as Maddox conceives it, should be an expression of the mission, economics, and life of the company. Expanding that idea, part of this approach is to encourage the employees to understand and to buy into this concept of brand identity and branded environments. Maddox has become especially concerned with how employees respond to brand identity when she realized that so much design is often disengaged from those who work in that environment. In order for people to understand that design was really an integral part of their work lives, it was essential that she demonstrate the connection of a pattern as it is lived in the work environment. To this idea she has added another component, the historical and cultural background in which her client organizations have evolved and developed.

To explore that added dimension to Branded Environments, in the 1990s, Maddox began teaching at the UIC (University of Illinois-Chicago Circle), choosing to go there to explore and develop the concept of patterning and strategies of how to play it out. As Maddox describes it, *Patterns are created when you mix the historical and cultural background of what you are designing, the literal design plan, and an element of surprise you want to bring into a design.*

Maddox became interested in patterning through cultural referencing and working with many different cultures and nationalities. The culture of patterning is taking that cultural referencing, the historical elements that could be brought forward in designing the plan that you are working with, and figuring out how that may or could manifest itself functionally. Maddox stayed at the University of Illinois for three years, working with students on patterning projects and documenting them along the way. She has used this method in her own firm, training and teaching students in the same process, and she has invented a design system which is based on her proprietary patterning theory.

RELENTLESS INNOVATION: DISCOVERING OPPORTUNITIES IN NEW INDUSTRIES

Maddox's modus operandi has always been never to turn down new opportunities, and she is fearless in accepting challenging, even seemingly impossible assignments. Over time, she became very interested in the area of health care. In the 1990s, she started working with the CCHMC (Cincinnati Children's Hospital Medical Center) and the Rehabilitation Institute of Chicago. Perhaps one of the most cutting-edge times of her career, the art program she designed for CCHMC was the first of several design contributions she would make in the health care industry over the next several years. CCHMC asked Maddox to develop a program which could make them distinctive and competitive in an expanded market with a new identity. The management team loved Maddox's pitch of building a story around learning, an educational program that would be beneficial to the patients, their families, and nursing staff alike. Since CCHMC specializes in oncology and treats many children with cancer, the idea of storytelling was important to the hospital experience, which usually included extended stays and repeated visits for the children and their parents. This project was a real crossroads in her career, and working with CCHMC enabled Maddox to take her business to the next level.

On the first project for CCHMC, Maddox designed everything to fit together in an "Our World" theme—murals, interactive exhibits, hospital curtains, uniforms, and wall and floor graphics—all designed to connect with the learning story and an environment friendly to children patients. It proved to Maddox that a visual storytelling element could be connected to design and the imagination of people could be captured to make them feel happier about living and working in this difficult environment.

Not surprisingly, a few years later, CCHMC asked EMA to design another building. By now, Maddox was extremely comfortable working in health care and she welcomed another project for Chicago's Rehabilitation Institute. To help generate new ideas, and with the encouragement of Dr. Henry Betts, now Chairman of the Rehabilitation Institute Foundation, Maddox spent a night in the hospital facility living the way a patient would—using the gurney, wheelchair, and other restrictive equipment. This way, she could understand and empathize with the wants and needs of rehab patients. With this personal experience, Maddox turned an idea on its head in the sense of providing a very stimulating and energized environment. Rather than it being labeled an "I can't" kind of place, it became an "I can" place with lots of color, light, and activity and with resources including libraries and videos. Far from it being a place of isolation, patients were encouraged to create their own social groups with activities being focused and visible in the center of the rooms rather than the outer edges to encourage greater integration and sociability among patients.

Her team designed the Center for Sports, Spine & Occupational Rehabilitation at the Rehab Institute, a combination of health club and medical facility. Probably the best rehab institute in the world, Maddox was lucky to have the opportunity to interpret her ideas and win the support of the institute's management team. One of the largest projects of her career, this $40 million package won major awards and led, not surprisingly, to future work at the Institute. Maddox continued to work on several other projects in health care including the Swedish Covenant Hospital. Her firm has become a leader in health care facility design, and, with that series of successes, she is now turning her ideas to design education.

Maddox's interest in education was concentrated on teaching people how to think about design. Teaching at UIC gave Maddox the impetus to start Archeworks in 1994 with Stanley Tigerman. According to the Web site, "Archeworks is an alternate design school where students work in multidisciplinary teams with nonprofit partners to create design solutions for social concerns" (Archeworks 2007). Archeworks is the culmination of the Branded Environments philosophy, combining a holistic concept of design with social concerns. This is a multidisciplinary design laboratory with a mission to develop prototype designs for health, education, and community. Students at Archeworks are not merely interior designers or architects. Archeworks draws from many disciplines, including lawyers, art historians, biologists, and experts in many other fields. Projects have included a delivery system for AIDS medication as well as environments for

Alzheimer's patients and their caregivers. Archeworks allows her to test and experiment—an important aspect because many times these ideas would not be considered by institutions unless they could actually be illustrated.

MENTORING AND RELATIONSHIP BUILDING

While in academia, Maddox also became a mentor to her students, a practice that continues today with students at Archeworks. Several of her protégés now have their own successful businesses. She cites a number of her pupils who have moved on to becoming entrepreneurs and running very successful enterprises. Recently, one of her students—a design director with a successful firm in Atlanta—came to see her and to work with Maddox after being away for ten years.

Considering that Maddox has worked for the last quarter of a century in what was a largely male-dominated profession, she has had to adjust her thinking. She is quick to point out that women in corporate America have to identify the links that men value so that they can leverage those links. She thinks that women have to be better in nearly every way, not just in basic skills but also in the ability to communicate and to work with other people. Women have the ability to take a holistic approach to their profession, not an easy thing to achieve. Discussing gender differences, Maddox concludes that there is something especially distinctive about women leaders. They are more engaged in personal relationships than men and, from a design point of view, they understand more about the intertwinings of design elements. Often, too, women are more willing to listen and respond directly to client interests and needs. Maddox has found that she can use a kind of "shorthand" with other women as they often just intuitively understand ideas without long explanations.

In 2002, after more than twenty-seven years, EMA was bought by Perkins +Will, one of the largest architectural firms in Chicago and in the United States. Perkins+Will has given Maddox, now a Design Principal at the firm, more resources and staff to expand Branded Environments, a concept she brought with her to this company. Today she directs this division of Perkins+Will, and it has grown under her leadership. Interestingly, although Perkins+Will is an old established firm, they have adopted Maddox's philosophy. She has become their thought leader, thus again acting both as an artist and as a leader in changing the mind-sets of her collaborators.

At Perkins+Will her team is designing the headquarters for Bank of America. They are in partnership with Haworth, Inc., one of the largest office furniture manufacturers in the world, in designing their showrooms and new corporate offices, all of which will combine beautiful spaces and furniture with environmentally sustainable products.

At Haworth, we believe that interiors should inspire—creating great spaces for the people who will work in them. Through appealing aesthetics, thoughtful ergonomics and a commitment to sustainability, our products aim to do just that.

Haworth's vision is thus closely aligned with Maddox's vision of Branded Environments.

Haworth is the only industry manufacturer to be a Malcolm Baldridge Quality Award finalist, the first in the industry to be certified by the International Organization for Standardization (ISO) 9000 for sustaining and improving quality in their products and ISO 14000 for creating products that reduce harm to the environment.

CHANGING THE WORLD OF DESIGN: THE LEGACY OF A LEADER

Eva Maddox has created a new idea, Branded Environments, which has changed our thinking and approach to interior design. This is her philosophy, and this holistic approach to design has become her lived story. She then elaborated on that story by developing a new focus on environmentally sustainable holistic design. She then propagated that vision through her work and teaching. She has used her enormous creative talent not merely to develop a new model for design. She has leveraged that idea into a highly successful business enterprise. Like many of the women in this book she has generously shared her ideas through the educational focus at UIC and in Archeworks. Few of us are truly creative; fewer are able to leverage what we love to do and are best at into a thriving commercial venture. Fewer still are willing to share their expertise generously to develop the talents of others. Eva Maddox is a rare person indeed.

She was voted one of the Chicagoans of the Year in 2002 by *Chicago Magazine,* named by *Fast Company* as one of the "change agents...designers and dreamers who are creating your future," and was the 2004 winner of "Woman Who Makes a Difference" award by the International Women's Forum. This year with a large staff from Perkins+Will she is tackling new projects and taking on new challenges while leading all of us into new ideas about design (Perkins+Will 2007).

REFERENCES

Archeworks. 2007. www.archeworks.org (accessed February 10, 2007).
Gardner, Howard, with Emma Laskin. 1995. *Leading Minds.* New York: Basic Books.
Haworth. 2007. www.haworth.com (accessed February 1, 2007).
Perkins+Will. 2007. http://www.perkinswill.com/people/people.aspx?g=design ers&p=maddoxe (accessed February 5, 2007).

Chapter 16

Customer-Centered Leadership and the Meaning of Success: Beth Pritchard

It all starts, begins and ends with the customer experience.

As *Fast Company* writer Jena McGregor puts it, "Too many CEOs are removed from their customer....[T]ruly customer-centric companies...do not delegate the customer experience to marketing or operations; it is a core function that has support at the highest levels of leadership. Leaders must be champions of the customer experience" (McGregor 2004). In fact, Anne Mulcahy has explained the turnaround she led at Xerox in the similar terms: "At Xerox, we got into trouble by losing sight of our customers, and we got out of trouble by focusing once again on our customers" (Mulcahy 2005). While CEO of Bath & Body Works, Beth Pritchard perfected customer-centered leadership using "creating an emotional connection with the customer" as her definition of success.

> *I want to make sure that we have the customer experience exactly right. It all starts, begins and ends with the customer experience. We need to have the right people in the stores and organization, and the right product assortment. The right customer experience embodies everything from what happens to them in the store to what happens as they're buying—it's global.*

BEYOND PRODUCT DEVELOPMENT: LEARNING TO MANAGE A BUSINESS

Pritchard extracted these insights about the centrality of the customer experience while growing up in two different business arenas—packaged goods and retail. After earning an MBA from Marquette University, Pritchard went to work in market research and product development for Johnson Wax, where she ultimately became vice president in the insect

Beth Pritchard

control division. During her time at Johnson, Pritchard learned the discipline of thorough and careful product development, a process that sometimes took as long as two years. On her own initiative, Pritchard also began to apprentice in business management with a top executive.

> *The experience gave me all different jobs across the company, international and domestic. But what he really taught me was how to manage. I could do my work at night and I would follow him to meetings during the day, and he would tell me why he made decisions and what he looked for. It was two years of the most incredible training—he was the mentor from heaven.*

With a solid grounding in product development and management learned over eighteen years with Johnson Wax, Pritchard switched to retail in 1991, soon becoming President and CEO of Bath & Body Works, a division of the Limited Brands. At the time, Bath & Body Works was just a fledgling collection of small shop alcoves in nine The Limited clothing stores. Yet by the time Pritchard moved on thirteen years later, Bath & Body Works had become a personal care chain with 1,600 stores, 35,000 regular season employees (65,000 during the holidays), and $2 billion in annual sales, making it one of the most successful retail concepts in that time period.

How did she build such a successful business? Attention to detail and thorough research, combined with a passion for customer intimacy and immediate feedback, fueled and accelerated Pritchard's professional interests and Bath & Body Works' fantastic growth.

I love being out in the stores with customers. I'm a very people person [sic]. What I don't enjoy is having to sit in an office reading report after report. I'd rather have someone come in, and we'll go through it together. You have to be able to make decisions quickly; you don't have the time or the luxury of knowing everything that's happening. In retail, your decisions are flanked by a lot of immediate information. I could turn to my computer and see exactly what sales were for all 1,600 stores, so if something wasn't working, we could react immediately, or if it was working, we could jump on the opportunity.

Comparing packaged goods and retail, Pritchard notes that the nature of the leadership between the two is different. She prefers retail because *You have to be able to integrate strategy and tactics into action plans much faster than in my previous life. And in retail, you have a direct relationship with the customer.*

Throughout her career, Pritchard has also had the opportunity to focus on the customer experience and build relationships with them through her products.

It all goes back to having to build that emotional connection with the customer. It's very difficult to get, and you can lose it in a moment. You cannot create a brand without emotional connection. You cannot create an emotional connection with a customer unless you face-to-face understand her. You really have to know what she believes in, know what she thinks about, and experience her same issues.

For Pritchard, it is not enough for sales associates and managers to be close to the customer; she expects it of everyone in the home office as well.

Every month all the key home office team members were out working at the stores, observing. I would stand at the cash wrap and ring out with the customers. We all had adopted stores. We talked to the store managers. You cannot run a business by anecdotes, so you also have to have research. We did a number of different things. Customers were given an incentive at every store to call in and give their impressions over a series of questions, and I could call up at any moment—I loved the immediacy— and hear what customers said yesterday about service. That really helped guide us.

While Pritchard continues to apply the same degree of intense focus on the customer that she developed at Bath & Body Works, she acknowledges *growth businesses are very different to manage than turn-arounds.... It's very challenging to fix other teams' mistakes. It's easier to fix your own messes because you know how you got into it.*

ETHICAL LEADERSHIP: COMMITMENT TO CUSTOMERS, EMPLOYEES, AND SHAREHOLDERS

Admitting to and fixing mistakes are important signs of integrity in Pritchard's book. For example, in the spirit of her commitment to customer service, during her days at Bath & Body Works, a new product had a problem with its label, but for Pritchard the issue became an opportunity to establish the brand's ethics, integrity, and transparency.

I remember one time we had a face care prize, and the label on the back was wrong. It was a reversal of ingredients in the inert area. It was very minor and did not have to be changed. But it was a new product, and I had them pull it because it had to make a statement of what we are all about. You can't start fudging on the little things, because then the big ones become easier and easier. We very firmly lay down what is our line in the sand, and you just don't cross it.

Not surprisingly, Pritchard applies the same standards of integrity to her own decision-making.

You have to be willing to make a decision. It may be a tough decision, it may be an easy decision, but as a leader you have to have the ability to step up and make that decision and then live with it. You also have to be able to admit when you made the wrong decision and very clearly say, "Hey, we're changing course. We tried this, but we made the wrong decision." Or, "at the time it might have been right, but it's not anymore, so we're changing."

For all her focus on customers, Pritchard is mindful of her responsibilities to employees and shareholders, particularly when they may be one in the same person.

There are a lot of people you have to think about. You have to be able to take very seriously the responsibility not only to your employees but to your shareholders. That's when as a leader you are the protector and the guide of shareholder value. There are thousands and thousands of shareholders. There may not be a lot of layers above me, but there are a lot of people you have to think about.

In a poignant example, Pritchard shared how this vast responsibility has a human face.

The first year I was at Bath & Body Works, I went to the distribution center, and there was a young woman I knew. She was a single mom and she came up to me and said "I want to know that you're going to be successful here." She was going to invest in some stock, two dollars every other week and wanted to make sure it was spent wisely. The weight of shoulders.

DEFINING PERSONAL AND PROFESSIONAL SUCCESS

Like many people, Pritchard's thoughts on the meaning of success to her family. Pritchard attributes her extraordinary drive to her mother. When Pritchard's father died, her mother had to become the sole bread-winner. As a nurse, Pritchard's mother worked two jobs, often putting in 16-hour days, working days, nights, and weekends.

> *She taught me so many good lessons. Be self-sufficient. You can love someone to death, but always be able to support yourself. Pride of accomplishment. So much of what I did was to make her proud as I saw how much she was working to give me a life.*

In retrospect, Pritchard observes that her definition of personal success has evolved in phases during her career.

> *Success has changed for me over the years. When I was at Johnson Wax, before I had our daughter, success was getting the deal done, being promoted faster. Success was defined in terms of title and salary. In my mid-years, when I was learning to go from mid-management to executive level, success was defined as being in an environment where I could grow personally and professionally, while still enjoying my family. Now success is providing opportunity and growth for many people. That's the thing I get the most joy out of. You can only buy so many toys, and you can buy only so many clothes. Now I can build a business not just because it makes a lot of money, but it's providing careers, which is wonderful.*

Meanwhile, Pritchard's husband, an attorney, has helped her maintain perspective about success. *It's rare to meet someone that can deal with driven women, and he's as strong as I am, but very supportive.* And of all the successes she wants, Pritchard says that *being a good mother, wife and friend are most important.*

The ideal organization, Pritchard imagines, is one where she and others will thrive, united around a common purpose and passion, but where they can also laugh, be irreverent, and have fun. *You have to get people that really commit to the same strategic direction. It really demands that you clearly communi-cate the overall goal, strategy and vision, but what makes it successful is the commitment of the people.* In that regard, Pritchard is a stickler for hiring very smart people who fit with the culture. (Whenever she is hiring, she asks herself the "test" question of whether she would want to sit next to this person on a plane ride to Europe.) For Pritchard, it boils down to this: *I don't want to work with turkeys. You have to be able to work hard, but you have to be able to laugh and let it go sometimes too.* And she means it. *I once had a woman who as a workaholic. She was good and talented, but I finally fired her because her people felt they had to do the same. They had no life working for her.*

Ultimately, Pritchard understands how her own example influences the tone of the organization and the behavior of others, and signals how to define success.

> *You have to emulate the spirit and the passion and the lifestyle you want in the office. I absolutely, totally believe in balance—balance what you have to do to get the work done and what you need as a normal human being. I've always said that and it doesn't resonate unless you demonstrate it. So everyone knows that if my daughter calls, you need to find me. If she had a lacrosse game, I would leave, but most importantly that gives them permission to do the same. You have to live it, you can't just say it.*

REFERENCES

McGregor, Jena. 2004. Putting customers first. *Fast Company*, no. 87:79.
Mulcahy, Anne. 2005. Anne Mulcahy on customers: You must make the connections. *Leadership Excellence*.

Chapter 17

Breaking Down Barriers in Executive Search: Barbara L. Provus

If I got a call for an assignment I knew that it was not because I was a female, it was almost in spite of being female that I would get the call. . . . So I thought if they're calling me it's because I do good work. . .and maybe I was somewhat more visible because I was a female.

Some believe that entrepreneurial ability is something you either have or you don't. Barbara Provus demonstrates that being in the right place at the right time may present an interesting opportunity, and entrepreneurship can mean recognizing the opportunity and following it through to a successful implementation. The ability to recognize the right opportunities to pursue, called "entrepreneurial alertness," is considered to be one of the fundamental behaviors of entrepreneurs (Gundry and Kickul 2007).

Provus achieved entrepreneurial success on her own terms. She was not about to ride on the coattails of other successful executive search professionals to build her reputation. Instead, she sets an example for aspiring entrepreneurs everywhere by making tough choices and seeing the results through to a profitable conclusion—in this case, her retained executive search firm: Shepherd, Bueschel & Provus, Inc.

FULL SPEED AHEAD: FROM SECRETARY TO PARTNER

Provus received her undergraduate degree from Russell Sage College where she earned her Bachelor of Arts in Sociology. Later she completed her Masters of Science in Industrial Relations with a focus on Personnel Management from Loyola University in Chicago.

When she graduated from Russell Sage College, Provus worked as a secretary for Booz Allen & Hamilton, a strategy and technology consulting firm. *Back in the early 70s if you were female and you had a college degree and*

Barbara L. Provus

you could type, you were hired as a secretary. The Administrative Assistant to the Chairman of the Board at the company became a mentor to Provus and guided her into the field of executive search: *She very much helped me to plan my career, and she's the one who got me into executive recruiting in the first place. She thought it would be a nice professional career for me.*

When Provus started in executive search at Booz Allen & Hamilton, there were very few women in the field:

> *I got [into the field] as a researcher, which was sort of going in through the back door, and it was really the only way women could get into [executive] search at that point. Today, almost 30 years later, it's a very different story. But even up until about the last five to ten years, seeing women professionals in the executive search field was the exception to the rule.*

Another role model to Provus was her mother, a homemaker who went back to work when Provus was in high school. Her mother had never gone to college and she got a job working as a secretary at the local high school. Provus saw her mother blossom as a result of the pride she took in her work. *I think maybe subconsciously that had a positive influence on me—that work could be more than just a salary; it could be a place of fulfillment.*

Provus worked through the ranks of the executive search field, achieving the position of Vice President in the Chicago office of a large national executive search firm. A turning point came when Provus found out that the firm would be put up for sale. Three of Provus' male colleagues decided that they were going to start their own firm and they offered her a place in the partnership, but Provus was torn.

The uncertain future of the national firm motivated Provus to seriously consider moving on. She really liked and trusted her three colleagues and she felt that their work ethic and work styles were highly compatible with her own. Her husband, Frederick Wackerle, had started his own executive search firm several years earlier and had been very successful. A conversation between Provus and Wackerle proved to be just the push she needed to make the leap:

> *When I was apprehensive, he said, "What's the worst thing that can happen?" I said, "Well, we might go out of business." He said, "Then what?" I said, "Then I'd have to find another job." And he said, "Do you think you would?" and I said, "Yes." Finally he said, "Then what's the worst thing that could happen?"*

Provus agreed that there was really no downside to starting her own firm, and that is when she decided to make the move. Still Provus says, *I never thought of myself as an entrepreneur.*

According to an article in *Entrepreneur* magazine, "In study after study, experts have concluded it is the courage to take the 'first step' that makes all the difference. This is the courage to launch in the direction of your goals, with no guarantee of success" (Tracy 2007). Provus decided to take the risk and strike out on her own with her male colleagues. She left the comfort of the established firm to try her hand at building a company based on her own ideals. Her clients had faith in her and her partners' ability to succeed and every existing client followed the group to the new firm.

BUILDING THE BUSINESS

As the new firm got started, the partners experienced setbacks due to their inexperience as business owners. For example, they didn't think of starting a line of credit since they had all worked for big firms in the past and never needed to worry about establishing credit for acquiring company resources. Without credit they were prevented from leasing phones from the local phone company and instead had to buy them—a costly lesson in the world of business ownership. *There were so many things that we took for granted— there were several days when we first started where we didn't have stationery, we didn't have phone service.* However, unlike many new ventures which struggle to make a profit, since all of their clients followed them to the new firm they not only had a client base but also revenue right from the start.

Despite the mostly successful transition into the new venture, Provus still doubted her ability to "pay her own way" by bringing in new clients: *I was very concerned that I wouldn't be able to generate enough revenue or work on enough assignments to really be equal in my eyes to the three guys [her partners] ... and ten, fifteen years later I'm one of the primary developers of business for our firm.* She now cites her prowess for business development as one of her greatest professional accomplishments.

Most of the firm's business comes through word of mouth. Provus works according to the principle that good work will bring in more work and this strategy has led to continued success for the business. She also believes that being a woman helped her build a strong reputation in the early years of her career when women were much less common in the field.

If I got a call for an assignment I knew that it was not because I was a female, it was almost in spite of being female that I would get the call. My conclusion was that no one was going to give me a search if they weren't comfortable working with women because most of my clients are senior level male executives. So I thought if they're calling me it's because I do good work...and maybe I was somewhat more visible because I was a female.

Provus does not name any formal professional mentors that helped her build her business, although she thanks her husband for his frequent advice—both solicited and unsolicited. As a retired professional in the same field, Provus says that while she appreciates his advice, she has worked *very* hard to have her own identity—even keeping her maiden name when they got married. Early on they did talk of working together, but Provus was just starting out and wanted to establish her own professional reputation separate from her already well-established husband. She says it was important to her to demonstrate that she had not achieved her reputation as a result of his prior successes. *He understood and respected that and has remained a mentor in a professional sense. He's a great gauge and guide for me in terms of having my own practice.*

VALUES OF A TRANSPARENT ORGANIZATION

Provus believes that her personal values were largely influenced by her secular upbringing. Her Protestant mother and Orthodox Jewish father chose to raise their children without a formal religious education. Provus explains how this influences her in her work today:

Growing up a lot of my values were just to do the right thing for the right reasons—not because someone's watching or you have to confess about it if you don't do it. Treating others the way you want to be treated and being able to look yourself in the mirror and know that there's nothing there that you're embarrassed about or that you're trying to hide from other people. The values of my organization are the same. My partners and I are on the same page in terms of ethics and integrity. We want everything in the way we run the firm to be transparent to our clients, and the same with our staff. We're very open and honest about everything that goes on in the office.

Provus and her partners also share the belief that the client comes first. They embody this mission by determining which partner is best suited to handle each search assignment, regardless of who received the call. Serving clients to the best of their ability also means sometimes having to turn away assignments to do the best quality work.

GIVING BACK: HELPING THE NEXT GENERATION OF WOMEN PROFESSIONALS

When asked if she sees herself as a mentor to others, Provus says, *Since we're not a large firm [mentoring] doesn't happen formally here, but I do try to give back some of the help that I have received over the years.* At the time of the interview, Shepherd, Bueschel & Provus only had three other female employees—two were administrative and one was a researcher. Provus has, however, spent time talking to women who want to get into the executive search field or women who are new in the field. She has also spoken to professional women's groups.

As for being considered a role model by others, Provus says it makes her feel old! She was named one of the Top 20 Women in search ten or fifteen years ago. *I will sometimes meet someone who says, "I've known of you for the last 20 years, I'm so happy to finally get to meet you!" and I'm sort of looking over my shoulder thinking, "who are they talking about? It can't be me?!"*

Reflecting on the intangible benefits of having her own firm, Provus says that it wasn't power or influence that she was looking for; instead, she cites the flexibility and independence that it allows: *Some days you may work twelve hours and some days you may work four. When you own your own business you're in charge and you can find the right balance.*

Provus retired in 2005 from Shepherd, Bueschel & Provus with over twenty-five years of experience in the field of executive search. She has served as a member of the Board of Directors at the Anti-Cruelty Society in Chicago (one of the largest humane societies in the country) for fifteen years, and as a member of the Board of Directors for The Chicago Network (an organization of professional women in Chicago who have reached the highest echelons of business, the arts, government, the professions, and academia) from 1995 to 2004, and served as Chair from 2002 to 2003. In her retirement, she serves as a Docent at Millennium Park in Chicago.

REFERENCES

Gundry, L. K., and J. R. Kickul. 2007. *Entrepreneurship strategy: Changing patterns in new venture creation, growth, and reinvention.* Thousand Oaks: Sage Publications, Inc.

Tracy, B. February 2007. 7 secrets to success. *Entrepreneur* 100.

Chapter 18

Leading a Learning Organization with Integrity: Martha Ries

The ideal organization is threat-free. Employees can raise issues without concern. It's trusting, where everyone is working together.

Martha Ries is Vice President, Ethics and Business Conduct for The Boeing Company. Boeing is the world's leading aerospace company and the largest manufacturer of commercial jetliners and military aircraft combined. The company's headquarters is in Chicago, IL, and the company employs over 150,000 people across the United States and in 70 countries. Ries has been in her current position for three years. She has a law degree and found that her legal background was a very good fit to the requirements of her position:

The legal thought processes can be different from the field of ethics, but this has actually been helpful. Although a given position on an issue may be legal, it may not be consistent with the company's values, and therefore not something we want to do.

In this position Ries is motivated by the opportunity to embrace new challenges.

My motto has always been, "Try new things." This is evident from my resume. Some people become experts in one area, but I prefer challenging myself to take on different types of assignments—to learn new things and to grow from these new experiences. Generally I can figure out how to do something unfamiliar and I don't mind change. In short—I like new experiences and change.

Martha Ries

While many leaders are willing to face the challenge of trying something new, still others are reluctant to confront the risks inherent in doing so. Most organizations seek to become innovative, and researchers have shown that the willingness and commitment on the part of senior management to be open to change is an important best practice of high-performing companies (Cooper, Edgett, and Kleinschmidt 2004).

As Ries explains,

You have to trust yourself that you can do the new things you set out to do. You have to have faith in yourself. Getting other people to trust you can also be a challenge. You have to help them to build that confidence in your abilities.

In an industry that has been traditionally male-dominated, with respect to the managerial ranks, Ries recounts that she does not believe she has ever been held back because she is as a woman.

There was no opportunity that was unavailable to me because I was a woman. You just have to be willing to work very hard. You have to learn how to say things so you will be heard and in a way that others will understand. You have to keep people involved. When I was in private practice I represented a major oil company, which was very engineering-focused and male-dominated. It was good training for what I do now. That experience helped me learn this thought process early.

EARLY INFLUENCES AND EXPERIENCES: THE VALUE OF PERSISTENCE AND TEAMWORK

Ries credits the many people who have helped her in her career, watched out for her, gave her opportunities, and trusted her. Both her present and previous bosses were role models. She said her family helped form her thought processes. She is from a large family of six children—five girls and one boy (the youngest). She recalled that her father always said, "You can achieve anything, you just have to do it. Once you choose, be sure to do it as well as you can." Education was a primary focus and expectation. All of her siblings have a strong liberal arts background. She believes this gave them all a different foundation from which to build.

Ries described some of the most significant events in her life that shaped her as a leader:

> When I was 16 I was an exchange student in Sweden. This enabled me to see the world from the perspective of another culture, and it was a transforming experience. Going to law school helped me to analyze information and helped me with my presentation skills. Arguments in front of judges have helped me in my current position, especially with speaking in front of employees.
>
> I was an athlete and played on a lot of sports teams. I did individual sports as well. I played soccer growing up, as well as field hockey and lacrosse. I played field hockey in college. Team sports help you understand what it means to be a part in the overall win, and to learn that being the star isn't as important as helping the team to win. You also learn to lose gracefully and you learn perseverance. There were several coaches that influenced me along the way. They taught me the importance of working hard and the value of training.

THE ROLE OF TRUST AND OPENNESS IN ETHICAL LEADERSHIP

Ries relies on her colleagues within her team to provide feedback to her, and to help her reflect on her beliefs and actions. Scholars have defined ethical leadership as "raising the bar" and helping people achieve their vision and dreams. According to Freeman et al. (2006), ethical leadership is:

> Helping people realize their hopes and dreams, creating value for stakeholders, and doing these tasks with the intensity and importance that "ethics" connotes. That said, there must be room for mistakes, for humor, and for a humanity that is sometimes missing in our current leaders. Ethical leaders are ordinary people who are living their lives as examples of making the world a better place while reaping benefits for themselves.
>
> (Freeman et al. 2006, 168)

Ries articulates the ways in which she encourages her team to share with her their honest ideas and reactions:

> *It's part of the job, for sure. When I teach at the Boeing Leadership Center I'm always thinking, am I acting as I should be? Am I doing things the right way? You have to look at yourself first. I ask my team to tell me if I'm off the mark! They can sense if something is wrong and you don't always know how you are being perceived. You have to have an understanding of where you can get in trouble and create an environment where people feel comfortable being direct and open.*

Ries shared that one of her greatest accomplishments is in helping create a work environment in which people are encouraged to ask for help, and to share information.

> *[We're] making it okay for people to ask questions—anonymously or not. We're still working on it, but the volume increase shows progress—over 20% per year growth. In the beginning, as a first step we did a lot of ethics training to get people to go to their Ethics managers for assistance as we built an open environment. Now as trust has built, we are transitioning people to go to their managers more. This is the beginning of a journey. I feel as we build an even more open environment this will help the company to grow.*

How has Ries determined if these initiatives are successful?

> *We are working to implement an "Integrity Index" to measure ethics more broadly within the culture. We plan to combine this with employee data to get a sense, culturally, how we're doing. We also have an internal dashboard metric that measures customer satisfaction and other statistics. We are learning to combine different types of data to get a more holistic view of the organization. We have also started to color-code the cases we receive to see where the problems are—this is a form of an integrated culture assessment.*

Ries describes her personal values as integrity, honesty, and growth.

> *I believe that self-accountability leads to growth. Courage—you have to stand up for yourself and say what you believe, even when it is hard or not convenient. Ethical questions strengthen my resolve to do the thing you think is right at the time, even if your opinion changes later.*
>
> *We stress integrity as an organization, as well as teamwork—people working together. Our focus now is on values and performance—they need to go hand in hand. This is a really important concept.*

Ries' views are aligned with contemporary views of an ethical leader, who: "not only holds her decisions and actions up to internal standards, but also incorporates societal mores and personal ethics. Ethical leadership moves the analysis of values and decisions from a test of internal consistency to an understanding within the organization's community standards and morals" (Freeman et al. 2006, 165).

Ries continues on to explain the connection between Boeing's mission and the day-to-day actions by which it is carried out.

> We have something called the 2016 Vision. [Boeing's 2016 Vision is "People working together as a global enterprise for aerospace leadership."] A customer focus is central to this vision, and it's completely consistent across the organization. When our new CEO arrived, he began to focus on leadership development. His leadership message was that everyone needs to be living the Boeing values and that leadership is integral to this. I try to make sure employees are holding themselves and others accountable for this vision—talking to direct reports about what we should be doing, and talking to direct reports about our business goals and objectives. I also work on teaching our executives how to apply our values in our high performance work environment. I also do this with our employees, as well as externally, to communicate how we have changed our program.

There are obstacles that must be overcome in any such leadership endeavor, and Ries acknowledges that communication can be a challenge, as it is likely to be in any global organization. People are located all over the world, and they won't always agree on all points. She underscores that it is important to communicate so that the message is heard. People collaborate and help each other quite a bit.

She described her own style of communication and her approach to employees in the following way:

> I have an informal style. I try to be approachable. I call people and try to create an environment where people feel they can call me and tell me things. I visit employees at their work locations to learn more about them and what challenges they may face.

LEADING BY FOSTERING EMPLOYEE GROWTH

Throughout the conversation, Ries talked often about her motivation to help employees develop and grow professionally within a learning organization. As a leader, she is oriented strongly to the needs of people, and she works arduously to create and sustain an environment in which people feel comfortable to express their concerns and ideas.

> I always wondered, "Could I lead an organization?" I wanted to know whether I could do this, that I could motivate people to move in one direction, to set a strategy. My passion is in leading people. I turned down positions that were geared toward just leading organizations. I wanted to help people grow.

The ideal organization is threat-free. Employees can raise issues without concern. It's trusting, where everyone is working together. The ideal organization is a growing organization from a learning perspective, always growing in new business. My personal goals are to keep growing and trying new things. I would like to write a book someday. Be a good parent, a good spouse, travel throughout the world. Enjoying what you're doing is key and somehow the rest follows.

REFERENCES

Cooper, R., S.J. Edgett, and E.J. Kleinschmidt. 2004. Benchmarking best NPD practices. *Research Technology Management* 47 (1): 31–43.

Freeman, R.E., K. Martin, B. Parmar, M. Cording, and P.H. Werhane. 2006. Leading through values and ethical principles. In *Inspiring Leaders*, ed. R.J. Burke and C.L. Cooper, 149–74. New York, NY: Routledge.

Chapter 19

Leading Change by Building a Culture of Trust and Communication: Desiree Rogers

I think you first have to be vulnerable to people. You have to be open to people. You have to be confident enough to show you don't know everything. This makes you an authentic leader.

Desiree Rogers is the President of Peoples Gas and North Shore Gas, the Illinois utilities of Integrys Corporation, and has been in this position since 2004. She has been at the organization for ten years, and prior to being elected as President, she served as the Senior Vice President of Customer Service. The companies she runs have approximately 2,000 employees.

Running a company is something that Rogers has always known she wanted to do. This role enabled her to influence the work environment for herself and others:

I think that for me to feel as if I am achieving something, it is important that I have the ability to work with others and overall, to be a part of establishing an environment where people are happy, people are doing great work, and people are achieving excellence. That's what I like to do.

Research on effective leaders has shown that they have vision, and know where they want to go and how to get there. Leaders excel at building teams, and value the skills and experiences of others (Banutu-Gomez 2006).

Desiree Rogers

MOVING FROM OUTSIDE TO INSIDE: THE NEWCOMER'S EXPERIENCE

When Rogers entered her firm, she was a newcomer to the industry. The company is over 150 years old and has a great history, with many long-term employees. Rogers described what it was like to come into the organization:

I came 10 years ago, and I was a lot different from the people that were here, because many of them had long tenures. They understood the gas business better than I did, certainly initially. And many of them had worked together for a long period of time. So I was the new kid in the sandbox, if you will, and with that comes a certain number of obstacles because you don't know how to play, you don't know who's who, and you don't know what positions other people are playing. And so you have to figure that out while playing the game. And then on top of that, you have to layer on individual personalities and the challenges of the business. I would say that the most difficult obstacle early on was probably just being the new person.

Research on newcomers in organizations has shown that entry is a time of sense making, reality shock, adaptation, and accommodation (Louis 1980; Schneider 1983). When newly hired employees or managers adjust effectively to the new organization, they are likely to report greater job satisfaction, commitment, values congruence, role clarity, task mastery, and fit (Bauer and Green 1998; Cable and Parsons 2001; Wanberg and

Kammeyer-Muller 2000), and organizations need to carefully consider the nature of interactions newcomers have with insiders to the company (Allen 2006).

To succeed in her position, Rogers worked extremely hard at understanding the business, and trying to familiarize herself with the relationships in the business. She had respect for the history, the culture, and the internal processes that existed in the organization. She felt confident enough to be a change agent. In organizations, individuals who are "change agents" usually assume the responsibility for managing activities associated with change (Banutu-Gomez 2006). They may serve in liaison roles among groups, departments, or levels in the organization to facilitate change. In describing her role as a change agent, Rogers acknowledges, *If you're going to be a change agent, you need to be certain that you understand what you're trying to change, as opposed to just changing for change's sake.*

MENTORS AND ROLE MODELS: A DIVERGENT PROFESSIONAL AND PERSONAL NETWORK

Rogers reflects on the benefits of the great education she received, starting down in New Orleans, then at Wellesley College, and then at the Harvard Business School.

I've been lucky to be at some of the best educational institutions in the country. They have definitely shaped my thinking. Part of the experience at both places is you are with such gifted people—people that are so bright and so driven, from all over the world. The group has been preselected by the institutions, and you quickly find out after you leave that the world is not quite like that. But, just the opportunity to be able to learn, think and study with some of the finest teachers in the States certainly makes an impact on you. Personally, it reiterates this whole idea of being passionate about excellence, doing what you can not to settle, and being a part of meaningful work.

Many individuals have offered advice and counsel to Rogers, including family members such as her mother, father, and grandmother, who she considers her role models. Rogers acknowledged that she finds it very helpful to have many people who will advise her when needed, although she doesn't necessarily consider modeling them. This lack of distinction among role models and mentors was common among the women we interviewed. Our leaders seemed to consider them as one and the same—people who have guided them and to whom they can turn to for advice and perspectives on a variety of issues in their work and in their lives. Within the wide network to which Rogers belongs, she mentioned her past Chairman as someone she can go to for counsel.

He has been with me pretty much since the beginning. Very early on I identified him as someone that I had a great deal of respect for, in terms of his values, his intellect, understanding of the business, [and] how he handled himself with people was certainly something that I admired. He was never selfish. He was certainly a person that I could hang my star on. Probably three months into my time here I knew that I wanted to work with and work for him.

When asked if she considered herself to be a mentor, Rogers replied that she helps where she can.

I don't have any formal process where I am mentoring someone, but I talk to people all the time about their careers and about how to handle difficult situations. I talk to employees about their concerns, what issues they might have, and their dreams—whether it's going back to school, moving to a new department, how to get a promotion, or whether or not this is the best place for them.

Similar to the responses of other leaders in the book, Rogers noted that she doesn't consider the advice and guidance she offers to others as being a "role model."

It's not something I ever really think about very much. From time to time if you're doing a public appearance, a speech or something like that, then you might think, "people are here to listen to what I have to say, it better be good," [but] I don't really think of myself in that way, or spend a lot of time thinking about it. I just do it—I am who I am.

LEADER AS CULTURE CHANGE AGENT: SHAPING VALUES AND ACTIONS

Desiree Rogers believes that her greatest accomplishment has been her efforts at culture change. She describes it as a "work-in-progress": When she came into the organization, she had a different view of the world, a different view of what things could be, and noted that she is continually cheerleading or talking about people taking ownership for the value they bring to the company. She believes that people should rejoice in what they do. She encourages them to say, "This is what I do and I do it very well." The dimensions of a collaborative culture include having the ability to ask questions and to probe, regardless of the level or position one holds. No one should be dictated to.

We're a team. All of us are working towards common goals. We need to strive to be less bureaucratic and more welcoming of all opinions. I feel that if people are happy at work, they are going to be happy when they get home and their families are going to be happier. All of that has tremendous potential in terms of what people can do, what they can accomplish, as opposed to a more bureaucratic, dictatorial type of environment. If we've all got to work, we may as well be happy while we're here!

One of the most difficult challenges is helping people to be open to cultural changes, and to reduce the likelihood of resistance to change. Research on organizational change has suggested that in preparing to cope with change, trust and openness are necessary between leaders and employees. As Banutu-Gomez (2006) noted, leaders who are willing to expose their weaknesses demonstrate that everyone will be accepted in spite of their weaknesses; when nothing is hidden, a tremendous energy is released and the organization can move forward.

Rogers reflects,

I think you first have to be vulnerable to people. You have to open up to people. You have to show, "I don't know everything—I'm the leader, but I don't know everything." I want to hear from people, I make mistakes. I need to correct them when I make them and not be shy about saying, "Yes, that was a mistake. That should not have been done that way." And then people start to see you as more like them, as opposed to some crowned deity that knows everything. That doesn't help anyone. That's not a good place to be. It's lonely. It's not interactive. You don't develop your interactions because people are thinking of you one way, instead of just as another team member; "I can't talk to her." It comes over time. You have to be patient. You can't force relationships.

Culture change is a deliberate process, and the results can be measured by observing people's interactions and behaviors. Leaders can identify if the change is going in the desired direction by paying attention to critical incidents that occur during the time of transition. Here is one example Rogers recalled:

One gentleman was just here about ten minutes ago. He was having problems in his job and had performance issues. His physical appearance is such that he can look threatening, and so to some extent people just assumed that he was. And maybe he fed into that, too, in his own way. And so he was really not very happy here. We were talking and I said, "You have to really work at turning this around, and you have to figure out what it is that you want, and not let anyone stand in the way of getting that." And now he's very happy. He has another position. He's doing well. He's a kind of ambassador—he's talking to other people, he's enjoying his work a lot more. As I say, you win one customer at a time; you also win one employee one at a time.

People are coming more into their own, understanding their work, understanding what the company's trying to do, what the goals are and how they fit in. We witness the rewards from this when we are successful, when we are able to excel. I think everyone wants to be, or aspires to be, part of a winning team. People like winners. Nobody likes losers. So you just keep that in mind, even for yourself. If you want people to like you? Be a winner. Rogers laughs when she says, *Don't walk around like a loser! Nobody will to come over to you.*

PERSONAL AND ORGANIZATIONAL VALUES: THE FOUNDATION OF CULTURE CHANGE

Desiree Rogers articulates her values as: *Trustworthy, honest, unselfish, hard-working, ethical. And I would also say just really focused on doing excellent work. I'm not willing to settle for the status quo, ever.*

She described her organization's values similarly: *Ethical, honest, hard-working, and trustworthy.* She explained the company's vision as seeking to improve the lives of customers by providing energy services. Leaders are symbolic, in that their day-to-day actions must embody the company's vision to help influence employees and to communicate how employees can carry out the vision in their daily work.

One of the most important roles of leaders, Rogers believes, is that they are continually looking for feedback on how the organization is doing. Are they serving their customers well? If not, what can they do to improve? What tools do they need to give to employees so that they can in fact deliver what they say they are going to deliver?

Rogers's view of how leaders can articulate and reinforce the company's vision and strategy underscores the importance of continually examining your progress, and making adjustments to be sure you accomplish what you set out to do:

> *You have the goals, you develop the tactics, strategy, and then you measure and monitor to make certain that you are, in fact, delivering on what you have promised. As you identify gaps, you try to plug those gaps. You try to make certain that you have analyzed what the root causes are so that you can address those and move on to the next ones. That's one thing you have to understand, it never ends. If you understand that, you're going to be OK.*

Leaders may confront obstacles during this process, as they attempt to carry out their leadership goals. Rogers acknowledges that there can be structural and communication impediments that can sometimes lead to misunderstandings or negative reactions. In many organizations, bottlenecks in communication can occur due to the way the organization and its departments are set up. Sometimes communication is misinterpreted, and people can err on the negative side. She advises people to *err on the positive side until you have a reason to be negative. Don't be negative first! Think positive.* Her approach with her employees is one that she describes as very comfortable, informal, direct, and professional. She wants them to feel they can be very open in the conversation at any point in time.

Rogers is very proud of her organization with respect to its ethical foundation. When asked if she has experienced any ethical dilemmas, she confidently replied that she has never had to worry about any problem like that. *If anything is even remotely not what it should be, it will be addressed and corrected and fixed.*

Rogers's reflections on leadership vision and what she strives for in her role are profound. As she remarks,

I wanted the ability to influence others. I think that is power. It is not something that should be taken lightly. It is not something that should be abused. It should be used in a constructive way, and earned. I would certainly say that it is something that I definitely aspired to. That's how I think you bring joy and create changes. You've got to have the ability to be able to do that. Without the influence and the power you're not going to be able to move.

How does she describe the "ideal" organization? *One where there is a clear vision, clear direction, and a brilliant team of leaders to have that vision come true.*

THE FUTURE: REENVISIONING PERSONAL AND PROFESSIONAL GOALS

Desiree Rogers' plans for the future include building in time for reflection on her work, and her life—to replenish the well, so to speak. This is crucial for leaders, both to avoid burnout and to retain the ability to envision new and challenging goals for themselves and for their organizations.

My goals are to ensure that I spend adequate time enjoying what I've achieved and doing some of the things that I want to do, as opposed to always working hard to please others. I'm in a position now where I can—and I am working on saying "no" much more often than I have in the past. Slowing down enough to see the details of life and not just rushing to the next thing. So often you can miss so much in between, and miss enjoying the details of life.

I want to make certain that I see the details and take time to think about them, enjoy them, walk places instead of always riding, take a few hours here and there, as opposed to packing my day with event after event, meeting after meeting—take some time to be able to think and reflect on the last meeting. That's not a waste of time. I'm working on this. I'm not there yet!

REFERENCES

Allen, D.G. 2006. Do organizational socialization tactics influence newcomer embeddedness and turnover? *Journal of Management* 32 (2): 237–56.

Banutu-Gomez, M.B. 2006. Great leaders know that all change must start at the top and the bottom: The whole human system must change. *Cambridge Business Review* 6 (1): 157–61.

Bauer, T.N., and S.G. Green. 1998. Testing the combined effects of newcomer information-seeking and manager behavior on socialization. *Journal of Applied Psychology* 83: 72–83.

Cable, D.M., and C.K. Parsons. 2001. Socialization tactics and person-organization fit. *Personnel Psychology* 54: 1–23.

Louis, M.R. 1980. Surprise and sense-making: What newcomers experience in entering unfamiliar organizational settings. *Administrative Science Quarterly* 25: 226–51.

Schneider, B. 1983. Interactional psychology and organizational behavior. In *Research in organizational behavior,* ed. L.L. Cummings and B.M. Staw. Vol. 5. Greenwich, CT: JAI Press.

Wanberg, C.R., and J.D. Kammeyer-Muller. 2000. Predictors and outcomes of proactivity in the socialization process. *Journal of Applied Psychology* 85: 373–85.

Chapter 20

A Passion to Achieve with Values-Laden Leadership: Paula A. Sneed

Things that I saw when I was a young child and when I was a teenager led me to believe that if you were in a position you didn't like or if things around you didn't make you happy, you could change them. That very simple philosophical belief really motivated me.

Paula Sneed recently retired as Executive Vice President, Global Marketing Resources & Initiatives for Kraft Foods, Inc. She worked for Kraft Foods for nearly thirty years. For her, this position was the pinnacle of a career throughout which she strived to reach the very top—and, she has achieved it with great determination. Kraft markets the world's favorite food and beverage brands including Kraft cheese, Jacobs and Maxwell House coffees, Nabisco cookies and crackers, Philadelphia cream cheese, Oscar Mayer meats, Post cereals, and Milka chocolates, to name but a few in more than 150 countries.

Sneed was named to this position in June 2005. She was responsible for worldwide leadership and oversight of Marketing Resources functions including Consumer Insights & Strategy, Media, Advertising, Digital and Consumer Relationship Marketing, Packaging and Brand Design, Consumer Promotions, Marketing Alliances, Kraft Kitchens, Consumer Relations, and other marketing disciplines for more than 100 major food brands.

Sneed joined General Foods Corporation (which later merged with Kraft Foods) in 1977 as an Assistant Product Manager. In 1980, she became a Product Manager in the Main Meal Division and then Category Manager for the Desserts Division in 1983. Three years later, she was appointed as Vice President of Consumer Affairs. In August 1990, Sneed became Senior Vice President of the company's Foodservice Division and one year later, she was named Executive Vice President and General Manager of the

Paula A. Sneed

Desserts Division. In January 1995, she became Kraft Foods Senior Vice President of Marketing Services. She was named to the additional post of Chief Marketing Officer in May 1999, where she was responsible for delivering world-class marketing across all of Kraft's marketing disciplines— approximately $1.5 billion in spending annually. In September 1999, Sneed was named Executive Vice President, Kraft Foods and President of eCommerce, helping develop and set the strategy for the company's newly created division. She became Group Vice President, Kraft Foods North America and President, eCommerce and Marketing Services in 2000. In January 2004, Sneed was named Senior Vice President of Global Marketing Resources.

THE MOTIVATION TO SUCCEED: EARLY INFLUENCES

Paula Sneed has relied on many individuals from whom she has learned throughout the course of her career. She was raised to believe that she could achieve whatever she decided she wanted to do:

> *I was very young when my parents gave me this sense that anything I worked hard enough for I could get—it was as simple as that. If you want something, work for it and you can get it. I'm a child of the Civil Rights era. Things that I saw when I was a young child and when I was a teenager led me to believe that if you were in a position you didn't like or if things around you didn't make you happy, you could change them. That very simple philosophical belief really motivated me.*

As a child of the Civil Rights era, her experiences led Sneed to believe that if you didn't like things around you, you could change them. This motivation pushed her in the direction of the public sector after graduating from Simmons College. After six years of working in the public sector, she decided to return to school. She obtained her MBA from Harvard Business School, initially thinking the experiences and training she received there would make her a better public policymaker and a better leader. However, she quickly realized that there were other career options open to her. Upon graduation she entered the corporate world, undeterred by the limited opportunities for women, and particularly for women of color at that time.

When I started graduate school I had no intention of being in private sector business; I wanted to be in the public sector. I had worked for six years in the public sector and only went to business school because I felt that the experiences and the training I would get would make me a better public policymaker and a better leader in the not-for-profit sector. In business school I found there were other career options that I didn't know about. Once I began working in private sector business, my thought was: "What are the opportunities for women like me?" At that point, the opportunity set for women, and particularly women of color, appeared very limited. My attitude was that anything you work hard enough for, you can get. So I set a goal of obtaining a position somewhere high up on the organization chart. I didn't have a clue how to reach it. I thought if I worked hard enough I might not get there, but I knew I'd get something better than I had that day. That was my motivation.

It was clear to Sneed that in the early years of her career, most of the men she was working with had never known African-American women as peers nor did they perceive them as their equals in the workplace. The first African-American member of Kraft Foods' management team, she excelled by developing a career plan and seeking mentors to help guide her. Early in her career at Kraft, she began telling executives during career discussions that one day she would like to run a major portion of the company. Sneed says of women, and particularly women of color: *We have to see ourselves as trailblazers. Racism and sexism are alive and well but they cannot become detractors.*

According to Catalyst's *2006 Census of Women Corporate Officers, Top Earners, and Directors of the Fortune 500*, women held just 15.6% of Fortune 500 corporate officer positions, down from 16.4% in 2005. The percentage of corporate officer positions held by women of color stagnated at 1.7%, as of 2005. Kraft, Inc. has placed special importance on diversity, and as of 2005, women occupied 31.2% of middle management and higher positions at Kraft on a worldwide basis. The company believes that measuring the representation of women in the ranks of middle management and above at Kraft worldwide is an important indicator of diversity, because women at this level serve as the primary source of female talent for the more senior management ranks of the future (www.Kraft.com).

VALUE-LADEN LESSONS: ON FAIRNESS, COURAGE, AND RESILIENCE

My mother and father always said work hard and you'll get rewarded. When you're a student that does happen. You work hard and if you earn an A, you get an A. But in business many times it really doesn't work like that. There were a number of things that I saw that just weren't "fair." I quickly learned that life's not "fair" but that fact shouldn't be a deterrent. You can make life more fair for yourself by the things that you do. That message really struck me.

Women have played a major role for Sneed throughout her life. Her earliest role models were her mother and godmother, who were devoted friends for fifty-one years. She grew up in a very close family with a supportive network of church and family friends around her. There was a lot of encouragement to be successful and to do well. As a young child, teachers and women at her church were doing things that she admired and wanted to accomplish. In her teens, Sneed learned a lot by watching civil rights leaders, quickly realizing that for her, the most important success factors were optimism, courage, and resilience.

I learned a lot by watching civil rights leaders about optimism, courage, and resilience. I reinforce to my 23 year-old daughter and other young adults that the most important factors for success are optimism, courage and resilience. You've got to be optimistic, no matter what happens in your life, no matter how bad things get, you've got to believe that tomorrow things can be better.

When I was a little kid and had a bad day in school, my mother would tell me, "Trust me, just go to bed and go to sleep. It will be better in the morning." Magically in the morning, it was better. It appeared better because the emotion and the energy around the negative situation were diffused by time. It's powerful to think that things will always be better, no matter how bad they are. You have to believe that there's a silver lining in every cloud.

I always have people that I admire, people who have some characteristics that I want to emulate. I'm a big believer in role models. I think if people don't have role models, they're really selling themselves short. They're not giving themselves the daily motivation that they need.

Sneed still remembers the story she read as a young businesswoman about a woman in her late thirties who was graduating from the Medical School at the University of Pennsylvania. Before the woman was 18 she had dropped out of high school, was a mother of two, in an abusive relationship. The young woman decided to get out of the marriage and, with the help of her parents, got her college degree and made it through Medical School. Even though Sneed didn't remember the young woman's name, the story stuck with her. When she read it she cut it out of the newspaper and pasted it on her refrigerator door with the words "Role Model" in big letters.

Sneed was lucky enough to also have a number of mentors in her life.

I have a concept that I call the "mentoring mosaic." It breaks the traditional mold about what a mentor is. People think, "If I'm a junior person I need to find a senior person to mentor me." In many situations the ideal senior executive isn't available. The mentoring mosaic is a group of people at different levels who can counsel and guide you.

A mentor is someone who thinks enough of you, and feels comfortable enough with you to give you feedback. Some people feel that unless they have a senior mentor, they're not going to get the benefits a mentor can provide. But many times people don't take advantage of the kind of mentoring that's right around them. Perhaps because they feel vulnerable, they don't want someone else—particularly a peer or a subordinate—to give them feedback. If you feel this way, you might not buy into the mentoring mosaic concept. But I believe it is easier to get a mentor if you broaden what you perceive a mentor to be and if you build yourself a mentoring mosaic.

Does Sneed consider herself to be a role model to others?

I didn't start out to be a role model, I started out to achieve things that would make me proud of myself and would allow me to live up to what my parents' aspirations were for me. When I was 16, I heard Martin Luther King's "I Have a Dream" speech delivered at the march on Washington. It was such an empowering time to be a black teenager because you really believed that the civil rights activists were making life better for you. Growing up, I thought things were going to be better in the future. I believed that I'd be able to do anything I wanted because of the progress made by the civil rights and the women's movements. If by my example I've encouraged other people to set higher aspirations, I am happy and proud.

Part of the reason women in my generation went into business careers was the opportunity to break down gender and racial barriers. I think some of my daughter's generation look at the things their parents did and the things they sacrificed, and these young women ask, "Do I really want to go through all of that?"

I remember late one Sunday night years ago I was in my study at home working while my daughter, then about 9, was reading in a little rocking chair. Suddenly she looked up and said, "You know Mom, I'm not going to go into business. I'm going to be a pediatrician." When I asked why she replied, "Irene's mother is a doctor and she doesn't work on Sunday night. She has off Wednesday, and she occasionally comes to school in the afternoon." At that point my daughter was comparing my schedule to a doctor's and, in her mind, my schedule was the loser. Now my daughter does plan on getting an MBA, but at that point she was not sure she wanted a business career based on the sacrifices one had to make to be successful.

Sneed is charismatic, and her personal values are integrated into her leadership approach. For her, these include respect for other people, maintaining humility, being charitable, putting others before you and turning the other cheek. She recalled a former coworker, Bob Bernstock: He was a couple of years ahead of me, but he was younger than I was. He was one of my first mentors. He told me if there were things I didn't like I should prove myself by doing a good job and getting promoted so that I could change things. Another sound piece of advice he gave her was to make a list of the characteristics she wanted to live by so that when *The Wall Street Journal* wrote about her, she would be proud of how they described her. She made the list. It included hard work, optimism, self-confidence, honesty, resilience, courage, being a reality changer, taking risks, being a lifetime learner, and being resourceful—all of which have stood her in good stead as she rose in the organization.

I truly think that the only way people can be successful is if they're grounded in who they are and what they stand for. Ethics and values are critical to sustained success in business. The best thing you can do for your children is to ground them in values and things that are really important. Give those roots a chance to settle and grow. That's what happened to me.

Friends, old and new, are fundamental to Sneed. She has worked hard at renewing friendships from her earlier years including those made in high school and college. For the last five years, a group of her friends have gathered for lunch during Thanksgiving weekend to reconnect. *When my husband first met these people he said to me, "Now I understand you." It's an eclectic group. Some of us were in elementary school together. We had a common bond, parents who worked very hard because they wanted to help their kids get someplace in life.*

Sneed's personal values have transferred easily to her leadership style at Kraft. As she describes,

I'm very open, very transparent, and I say what I think. My motivating thought is that I can do anything I want to do—not arrogantly—but I fundamentally believe that. I know I'm going to work hard in any assignment. I'll do my best. I'm competitive, but not negatively competitive.

Sneed enthusiastically talked about the mission at Kraft, and what she believed her role to be in contributing to this mission:

We have the mission of being the undisputed leader in branded food products. We want to help the world eat and live better. Kraft's values are: focus, innovation, trust, passion, teamwork and speed. Quite honestly, I love the fact that we want to be the undisputed leader and that we want to help the world eat and live better. It is very consistent with my personal values.

In my group we have the opportunity to help the company deliver world-class marketing. Whether it's advertising, promotion, media, packaging, or

marketing insights and strategies, my challenge to my group is to deliver "Nothing short of world-class marketing that will grow Kraft's top and bottom line." I feel terrific about our contribution to Kraft.

In certain aspects of marketing, we are the undisputed leader. We've got the best consumer-focused Web site in all of packaged goods, Kraftfoods.com. We have a consumer relationship marketing program where we publish a magazine, "Food and Family," that's distributed throughout North America to 12 million households five times per year. It is the number one French language magazine, the number one Spanish language magazine, and the number two English language magazine in North America. Reader's Digest and TV Guide are the only other magazines with higher circulation. "Food and Family" has won all kinds of awards. I feel great about those marketing tactics. For someone who likes the thrill of the chase, this is a perfect job for me.

When I first came into Kraft I wanted to be a general manager. There had never been a female general manager. In fact, there had never been a black woman promoted above the first level in marketing. Between the first level and the GM level was something like nine positions. I set my sights on the GM position, recognizing I needed a big goal. That dream fueled hard work. When I first started, I had doubts if there would be a woman promoted to GM during my career, but I knew that if I didn't work for it, I wouldn't achieve the goal. The hard work paid off. I got to GM and made it to even higher positions. Over the past 25 years women have broken through the glass ceiling because they believed through their hard work and by delivering results they could change the reality of the corporate environment.

MOTIVATION TO LEAD: THE ROLES OF POWER, INFLUENCE, AND SERVICE

Was power important to Sneed? She prefers to say it was an important motivator and that she followed her mother's example. Her mother was always a leader in the church and the community. Sneed soon realized that if you can be the president of something, why wouldn't you be? She began leading early in life as president of her class in junior high school. She has always enjoyed leadership. *I would always get frustrated if I got into a situation and things weren't well-organized and running well. I think more women than men are perfectionists—but most women are collaborative consensus building leaders.*

Sneed believes power should be used very wisely, and her best example of what power should be is *a leader should be a servant. If a leader is not a servant in some meaningful way then they're not a good leader. A leader needs to encourage people to reach a higher level of performance than they could imagine.*

She admits that in the last fifteen years, corporate life in America has been more disheartening with downsizing, outsourcing, and mergers, much of which has come as a result of slower growth, she notes. When she was coming up the ranks, companies were growing more quickly. Sneed believes that now more than ever leaders need to be close to people, clear about the present, with aspirations about the future. She worries that *some leaders are* too short-term focused and don't make tough decisions that will build companies in the long term.

She is at the front end of the baby boomer generation, and noted that many people of her age are retiring or leaving corporate roles. As she thinks about her future, she would enjoy the challenge of working for a smaller company, a not-for-profit, or an educational institution. As she thinks about her career and life experiences, she explained her philosophy:

I decided early on that I wanted to be married, to have children and to pursue a successful career. It is not easy for women to have a good, happy, healthy marriage and to raise kids, and climb the corporate ladder. While all of those things are possible, doing them together at times can be difficult. It requires planning and compromise. It requires real thoughtful decision making about what is important, what your priorities are, and being decisive on how to get things done.

One piece of advice I give to younger women when they begin thinking about business careers is to think holistically about what you want in your life and to make good choices in partners, because unless your personal life is in order and happy, it's very tough to manage all the complexities of a professional life. For the first few years, it's fine, but about ten years into a career when you're managing career, marriage and family, it can get tough.

A lot of women get frustrated by the tensions and the complications. But by doing long-term planning and by being clear about what you want, you can handle the tensions successfully.

I took this course my second year in business school called Self-Assessment and Career Development. In one exercise, you drew a picture of what your life was like as a student, and another picture of what you wanted your life to be like in 10 years. Your personal plan and your career plan were the bridges between those two pictures. I liked the idea that I should give careful consideration to my life plan, just as I had been taught to give careful consideration to business planning. As a result, my husband and I spent a lot of time talking about our life and career plans and our goals. We talked about how we would make the life and career plans happen. It made things a lot easier when we were facing pivotal points in our lives. We still have plans we are implementing. When you have life plans, you can always change them if necessary, but the problem is many people don't have life plans—so they flounder. Women especially need life plans and they need to be diligent in thinking through and communicating what their dreams and aspirations are and how they will go after them.

REFERENCES

Catalyst. 2007. 2006 Catalyst Census of Women Corporate Officers, Top Earners, and Directors of the Fortune 500. http://www.catalyst.org/pressroom/press_releases/2006_Census_Release.pdf (accessed March 14, 2007).

Catalyst. 2006. 2005 Catalyst Census of Women Corporate Officers, Top Earners, and Directors of the Fortune 500. New York: Catalyst.

www.Kraft.com. Diversity. People. http://164.109.46.215/responsibility/people_diversity.aspx (accessed March 15, 2007).

Chapter 21

Managing Reputation the Right Way: Pamela Strobel

Are you always taking the high road?

CORPORATE REPUTATION: BASED IN VALUES

Corporate reputation is more important than ever in today's low-trust, scandalous environment, and companies stand to gain sales, among other things, when their corporate reputation is high (Harris Interactive 2007). Although many companies have overlooked the importance of corporate reputation, some recognize it as a corporate asset. The Corporate Reputation Quotient of Harris-Fombrun identifies six drivers of corporate reputation as follows: emotional appeal, products and services, vision and leadership, workplace environment, financial performance, and social responsibility (Reputation Institute 2007).

Pamela Strobel is a leader who recognizes the importance of reputation management, and not only for what it can do for Exelon, where she served in a top leadership position, although that is important. Reputation Management is an initiative that Strobel led which is consistent with her values and ethics, as well as the culture of the organization. Many companies want to lead with integrity, but have difficulty *making that real*, according to Strobel. Strobel, however, insists on *always taking the high road*, as she recognizes how easily an organization's reputation can be lost. Her upbringing, values, and role models made it natural for her to practice what she preaches as a leader.

RISE TO THE TOP

If there is one woman who has made it in a male-dominated world, it is Pamela Strobel. As the former Executive Vice President and Chief Administrative Officer of Exelon, she has made inroads in an industry that has

Pamela Strobel

traditionally been dominated by men. Exelon was formed in 2000 when Unicom (the parent company of Commonwealth Edison in Chicago) merged with PECO Energy in Philadelphia. Exelon is now the largest electric and gas utility company in the United States.

In some respects, Strobel happened to be in the right place at the right time. Having gained an undergraduate degree in journalism, followed by a law degree from the University of Illinois, she originally joined Commonwealth Edison, otherwise known as ComEd, in 1993 as General Counsel. She was persuaded to move to ComEd from Sidley & Austin—where she was a partner—by the then-President of ComEd, Sam Skinner. It wasn't too long before Strobel rose to the position of CEO of the energy delivery side of ComEd.

In 1998, John Rowe became the new CEO of Exelon and, having decided that a merger was in the cards, asked Strobel if she would be interested in leaving the legal world behind and taking on more of an operational role. Although she did not actively seek the position, Strobel was excited about the challenge and felt the timing was right. The challenges were certainly there. In a speech she gave in Washington DC in 2000, she discussed some of the things she had to meet head-on in this new role: an aging infrastructure compounded by neglect; outdated design contrasted with unanticipated growth and meeting a national commitment to universal service. Add increased competition to the mix and it is amazing that Strobel could remain so positive and optimistic in the years ahead.

However, all this stood her in good stead as in late April 2003, Strobel assumed her role as Executive Vice President and Chief Administrative Officer when the company was reorganized. It gave her the opportunity to work in a more corporate position where she could demonstrate her

commitment to meeting customers' expectations for relia
more innovative ways of working with those customers
business needs.

So how does Strobel survive in this incredibly male world? She is u..
to point out that she strives to give the best of herself every single working
day—a quality she also expects from her team.

> *If a person does the very best job that he or she can, and you actually look at
> that job as an opportunity for you to make a contribution, each day you come
> in and you know you can do more. I've always looked at the world that way—
> doing your best every single day.*

Her philosophy emphasizes that each day presents new challenges and new
opportunities when each individual really feels that they can do more.
Strobel also notes that *I am a very practical person, logical, and work-oriented;
I'm always doing something, I'm always taking on tasks, so I'm kind of action-
oriented.*

She describes her working day almost as a voyage of discovery—finding
new things that need to be done and new ways of doing them, determining
if it is the best way to do them. Strobel points out that, with this philosophy,
individuals get noticed since the majority of people do not approach
their working day in this way. Therefore, new jobs, new positions, new
opportunities present themselves almost as a matter of course.

This has certainly been the path that has led Strobel to her present
position. *And that's how I like to pluck people that I'm seeing who are growing
up in their positions. I'm looking for attitude and intelligence and motivation
and hard work—a real willingness to work hard. And if I see that in other people . . .
they can do about anything.* In Strobel's opinion, with these traits and
behaviors, an individual could work in just about any department and in
any position.

POWERFUL ROLE MODELS

Looking back, Strobel's constant striving probably stems from her grandmother. An amazing role model for Strobel, her grandmother was the first
woman to get a degree in physics from the University of Illinois back in
1918. She went on to get her master's degree in physics, and her first job
was at ComEd in the early 1920s.

It was fascinating and instructive to Strobel that, in 1920, there was no
better place in the world to work because you were part of bringing the most
important thing into people's lives—electricity. It was changing the world
and to be working at ComEd was, according to her grandmother, tremen-
dously exciting. High growth, energized and extremely satisfied employees
were the order of the day under the leadership of Samuel Insull, then the
preeminent utility manager in the United States. Everyone loved each
day's work, and the contribution being made to society was outstanding.

Over time, that euphoria got lost as the company, in the depressing 1930s, encountered severe challenges.

Role models don't come better than Strobel's grandmother. *I've had a lot of great people to model myself after but my grandmother is my personal role model.* Strobel's grandmother lived until 1999 which allowed Strobel six years of sharing what she was living through at ComEd and comparing it with her grandmother's experiences. Strobel's grandmother modeled many leadership behaviors, and Strobel shared several examples of these.

> *She ran for the Clerk of the Circuit Court because she thought someone needed to do the job better. She raised all the money for a new wing on her church because they needed it; nobody else said they could raise the money and she said "Alright, I'll do it." She traveled to every country in the world, and learned how to use a computer in her nineties.*

Strobel certainly appears to have inherited her grandmother's practicality, curiosity, and constant pushing of the boundaries. *When I go back to how you approach each day, that would be my grandmother. "Everyday there's more to do; let's do it." She always said never put off until tomorrow what can be done today. So, I live my life that way.*

Strobel considers herself fortunate to have worked for some other great role models in her journey up the ladder. Dick Ogilvie, who at one time was the Governor of Illinois, was running the law firm where she practiced from 1977 to 1988. She describes him as a wonderful mentor and an outstanding leader. *If I took something away from Dick Ogilvie it was, make decisions. Just face up to decisions that need to be made.* Strobel is grateful that he opened a lot of doors for her and facilitated opportunities for her to pursue.

Strobel also continues to admire two men she has worked with at Exelon. She cites Sam Skinner, former President of ComEd, as someone with tremendous energy, always taking on new things and possessing a wonderful sense of humor. Another mentor she discusses is Jim O'Connor, the former chairman and CEO, who spends considerable time contributing to countless charities in Chicago. John Rowe is another outstanding manager who is analytical and an excellent visionary. Having worked with incredibly bright people, she is determined to mentor and grow the team she has around her.

Strobel readily agrees that she has had a lot of luck along the way and counts herself fortunate not to have encountered many obstacles in her career. Married with two children, assumptions might have been made that prevented her from being considered for certain positions. She has always said that you should give someone *the opportunity to say "No, I can't do that right now." Don't assume it away from them.*

MENTORING FOR WOMEN

Although Strobel does not have a formal mentoring relationship, she takes very seriously the fact that there are not too many women in high executive positions. *It's just a fact of life when we look at the statistics and so I take it as . . . it's an obligation, almost, to make yourself available to women.* Often getting e-mails and calls, Strobel does not turn down requests to spend time with a woman, or network with one. She was also very involved in starting a women's group within Exelon, and she often talks to women's organizations. Strobel believes that many women would consider her a mentor to them because they can go to her with their problems, and she offers them good career advice.

A cause dear to her heart, Strobel's goal is *wanting women to succeed. I want there to be many more women who stick around in companies so it's not an anomaly that we have women in high places—it's just more and more the norm.* She often gets requests from women who have been casualties of downsizing within a business or who have come to a career crossroads in their life, and Strobel always strives to help these women. She also tries to help women present themselves in the best possible way; when Strobel thinks a woman can benefit from some coaching on say, her presentation or other communication skills, Strobel asks the woman if she can offer some feedback.

ALWAYS TAKING THE HIGH ROAD

Ever the pioneer, Strobel led an initiative at Exelon called "Reputation Management." Stemming from her values of honesty and integrity, this initiative is one that she believes many companies are undertaking today.

> *They're recognizing that a corporation has a reputation the same way a person has a reputation. You build your reputation over time, day-in and day-out by all of the activities that you undertake and all of the things that people see you do, just like we do as individuals. You can be good, good, good, but then some Friday you're very bad and that's going to hurt your reputation. You can lose it all in a very short time.*

Strobel believes that although many companies talk about corporate values, and every company cites "integrity" as one of them, all of the companies do not really put their values into practice. How do you make values real?

> *They should be something that you are actually talking about as you're making a decision. "Are you always taking the high road?" I use that phrase. I overuse that phrase with people, but it always makes the point [that] we're going to take the high road. We're not going to overly criticize. We're not going to hide, ever. We're going to be known for our openness.*

Strobel demonstrates consistency in words and deeds, which according to Kouzes and Posner (2003) is the ultimate measure of credibility, the foundation of leadership. "Model the Way" is one of their exemplary practices of leadership and occurs when personal actions are aligned with shared values. Another example of her absolute belief in these values is the fact that *honesty and integrity are the things I talk about the most with my children*. They were important in Strobel's youth as well.

Even as a teenager, Strobel was not good at keeping secrets. She thought it was a bad thing, and also bad to talk about people behind their backs. She remembers that she would be the one to *let the cat out of the bag*, forgetting that something was supposed to be kept secret. Later on as a lawyer, she realized that there are situations where it is important to be protective of information, and she viewed things somewhat differently. Today she is pleased to be in an environment where full disclosure and openness is part of the everyday culture, as it is important for the sake of the company and reputations, both corporate and individual. She credits John Rowe, Exelon's CEO, for modeling his values of openness and honesty; his reputation for this helps those values permeate the company. It is the role modeling on the part of leaders and key individuals, especially during critical incidents (Schein 1985) that will continually remind organizational members of the values that keep their culture strong.

FUTURE CHANGE LEADERSHIP AND PERSONAL GOALS

What does the future hold for Strobel? At the time of our interview she didn't foresee huge obstacles in meeting Exelon's business objectives, but there was still "much to accomplish" in the area of change management. *We've reorganized the structure of the company over the last year or so...we still have obstacles around silos of people, or people in one part of the company used to doing things in a particular way, [who are] not accepting change, organizational change, as easily as others.* At the time, Strobel saw her role as connecting people and bringing parts of the organization together to achieve greater efficiency and value to the customer. How did she plan to do this? Not surprisingly, the openness value played a major role. *We're still working really hard at getting better—improving communication and information sharing across the whole corporation.*

The ability to have influence has motivated Strobel in the past to achieve higher positions in her career, and her attained positions have increased her levels of influence. Yet Strobel is uncomfortable sounding like she may be bragging or promoting herself. In this regard, Strobel might be considered a "Level 5 Leader" (Collins 2001) for her ability to display the rare combination of humility with strong will in her leadership. She believes that women may be more uncomfortable than men with self-promotion, although she admires the men who are also humble regarding their success.

When Strobel addresses identity issues, she recognizes that she does not

get my core feeling of who I am and what I am from the job position I have. I'm lucky that way. On the other hand, sitting here with that job position, I know that I can help the United Way in a more important way. I can help the Joffrey Ballet, which I chair the board of, in a different way. I can make phone calls that I wouldn't be able to make otherwise.

In conclusion, Strobel notes that the ability to influence is a factor that is there, but that it does not define who she is.

When asked about her future goals, *happiness* is a quick response from Strobel.

You can get that from your job, you can get it from your family, you can get it from your friends, you can get it from the not-for-profit things that you do that are helping other people. Most importantly, you should probably get it from all of those things. Life is short and as long as we recognize the various sources of happiness, we should say that is my number one goal.

REFERENCES

Collins, J. 2001. Level 5 leadership: The triumph of humility and fierce resolve. *Harvard Business Review* 79 (1): 67–76.

Harris Interactive. 2007. *Corporate reputation.* Retrieved March 21, 2007. http://www.harrisinteractive.com/services/reputation.asp.

Kouzes, J.M., and B.Z. Posner. 2003. *The five practices of exemplary leadership.* San Francisco: Pfeiffer, A Wiley Imprint.

Reputation Institute. 2007. *Corporate reputation quotient.* Retrieved March 21, 2007. http://www.valuebasedmanagement.net/methods_corporate_reputation_quotient.html.

Schein, E. 1985. *Organizational culture and leadership.* San Francisco: Jossey-Bass.

Chapter 22

Leading a Learning Organization: Donna F. Zarcone

The day you stop learning and growing is the day you start dying.

A LOVE FOR LEADING AND GROWTH

Not many CEOs come to work every day with a smile on their face—but Donna Zarcone does. As President and COO of HDFS (Harley-Davidson Financial Services), she is at the top of her game thanks to her persuasive and negotiating skills and a solid strategy of knowing exactly what she wanted from the beginning of her career.

My motivation was to be able to lead. I love to grow organizations, I love to develop people, I love to garden, that's just who I am. I love to lead, it's very energizing for me to be able to take a group of people, build a team, set a common purpose for that team to accomplish, and then go and make it happen. I enjoy being a part of that, whether it's problem-solving, leadership development, communication with employees or all the different aspects of understanding and working with customers. It gives me a high level of personal satisfaction.

She landed the top job at HDFS in 1998 having previously served as Vice President and CFO for four years. She worked very closely with the founder of HDFS, Steven F. Deli, who was in the process of taking a small company and dynamically growing it. Deli, a former investor banker, was in need of a leader with business operations expertise, so he hired Zarcone who had a history of helping companies grow. The primary focus of HDFS is to provide wholesale and retail financing, credit card and insurance services to dealers and customers of Harley-Davidson, Inc. It was established as an independent start-up in 1992 and was subsequently acquired by Harley-Davidson, Inc. in 1995.

Donna F. Zarcone

Some years later, Deli announced his decision to leave the company and, as Zarcone had partnered with him throughout her career at HDFS, she was the Board's natural choice as his successor. Her responsibilities included establishing business strategy and providing operational direction and oversight to achieve strategic and financial results. She represented HDFS to its dealers, customers, the financial community, and the general public. From 1998 to 2006, during her eight-year tenure as President, the company's annual operating income grew from $20 million to over $200 million and its managed loan portfolio grew from $1.1 billion to over $6 billion.

In fact, Zarcone feels that one of her greatest accomplishments has been to grow the HDFS organization from a small start-up operation to one with 750 employees and great jobs. *We've done so by creating a good organization...we have employees who contribute and make a difference. That's very rewarding... developing what I believe to be a very fine company.* Feedback from both employees and customers is very positive; employee satisfaction is high and customers' needs are being met.

LEARNING TO LEAD

But let us go back to the beginning. Donna Zarcone graduated from Illinois State University at Bloomington-Normal in 1979. Her first position was as a young accountant at Peat Marwick Mitchell, and one of her first assignments was to conduct the first year audit for NF Computer Sales & Leasing Corp. (NFC) run by two former IBM salespeople. *They were entrepreneurs and we had to completely redo their cash-basis books to convert to GAAP accounting. However, at the same time, they wanted to learn all they could about lease accounting so I ended up teaching them.* Zarcone gave such an impressive performance at NFC that it was not long before they offered her the position of controller, knowing that she knew more about the accounting side of the business than they did! It was her first experience at risk-taking—should she play safe and stay with the security of Peat Marwick or reach out and join a small, new company and see where it took her? Not surprisingly, she chose the latter and has never looked back.

The move proved to be not only a teaching experience for Zarcone, and she recognized that although she may have been a partner at Peat Marwick some day, there was a worthwhile learning experience to be had as the nineteenth employee of this small company that had begun in the basement of the two founders' house. *I thought they would be great entrepreneurs some day and I wanted to learn from them; they were growing a business and they were so passionate about it. I really wanted to understand and learn. In the end, they proved to be great teachers and very successful businessmen.* Ever the ambitious one, Zarcone decided that if she was really going to reach for the top, she needed to pursue an MBA. *They agreed to pay for my Master's so I went to the University of Chicago at night while working for them.* So, while spending her working day at NFC, Zarcone studied for an MBA in finance and earned her degree in 1987. Zarcone fondly recalls that NFC's owners so believed in her that they put her through a number of coaching programs, including Steven Covey's leadership program (before he became famous!); this helped her develop her leadership style.

Apart from clearly having the innate abilities to be a great leader and manager, Zarcone always soaked up information and was prepared to learn from others. She talks in detail about one of her bosses at NFC. *He was a genius; he had a photographic memory, understood detail, understood risk, and understood the structure of transactions in a way that made him a wonderful teacher. He would say, you're looking at it wrong—this is how you should look at it. He took me under his wing and really helped me understand and learn.* Although he was making excellent business decisions, his management style not as refined. By contrast, his business partner was a great salesperson and *one of the best people guys I've ever worked for, truly an inspirational leader,. . .people would go through the wall for him.*

The entrepreneurial spirit she experienced at NFC supported Zarcone's achievement orientation. *It was an entrepreneurial organization so it didn't matter how old you were; it didn't matter if you were a man or a woman—all that mattered was that you produced results. And if you were producing, you were growing and so at 28 I was VP of Finance and at 32 I had the whole back office.* She became the Executive Vice President and CFO with responsibility for accounting, treasury, legal, information systems, and other administrative areas at NFC. In the same year that she earned her MBA—1987—NFC's

owners sold their company to a subsidiary of Chrysler Financial Corporation, and Zarcone found herself sitting on the board of Chrysler Systems
Leasing, Inc. as Vice President.

Zarcone is proud to say that those original managers from NFC in the
1980s remain her great friends and mentors today. *When I'm making career
decisions today, I call them up and they will tell me, "What, are you nuts?"...or
they'll say "That's a great idea," or "Perhaps you should think about it this way."
What's special about having them still as advisors today is that they are so candid
with me; everybody should have somebody who can do that for them.*

From Mentee to Mentor

Having gained and learned so much from others, it would be easy to
understand if Zarcone had a formal mentoring program in HDFS. But she
doesn't. She prefers to nurture and develop her staff in her own informal
way, and she gives examples of two individuals in HDFS who she has taken
under her wing.

Zarcone is quick to notice potential and knew that one of her financial
analysts had it. She worked with this individual to have him reach a whole
different level of performance by providing feedback that he was willing to
hear. Zarcone's coaching convinced him to invest in himself and continue
to learn and grow, and it paid off. Today, he is Harley-Davidson, Inc.'s Vice
President and Treasurer, and well regarded in the industry as he has rapidly
moved up the ladder. *I think that's an important part of a leader...to be a teacher
and grow new stars,* Zarcone explains.

Another of her protégées started out in the company as the receptionist.
*Norma was willing to learn and grow, so over the years we sent her to a number of
programs and seminars, including leadership classes. Now she's our office manager
as well as my executive assistant. She manages the office, has two direct reports and
she has mentored at least another 3 or 4 people.* Perhaps the ultimate sign of her
development, Norma herself is now growing into a leader, and has coached
and groomed a number of staff in the office. Zarcone says of Norma: *She's a
great representative for our company, she believes in herself and she's been willing
to grow and learn.* Zarcone tells these stories about her coaching successes
with great pride. *Seeing people succeed here is very fulfilling. Occasionally we lose
a good employee to another great opportunity, and while I'd like to keep them, if they
go someplace else and thrive as a leader, that is still a positive reflection on HDFS.*

LEADING IN A LEARNING ORGANIZATION

Zarcone is very passionate, loves to grow organizations, and has the ener-
getic personality of a born leader. She is highly motivated and encourages
her team to be the same. Zarcone certainly believes in her company, her
employees, and her product—she even has her own Harley-Davidson
motorcycle! Her leadership at HDFS stems from her personal values of
integrity, fairness, and equity; she constantly asks herself if she is doing the

right thing for the company. Zarcone understands the importance of these values in getting belief and buy-in from followers. *If you do the right thing, it will feel right, people will see it, you'll be able to explain it, and people will follow you because they believe in you and the values you represent.* Her ideal organization *respects its people and encourages active participation from its employees, lives its values, achieves goals and objectives, is close to the customer and exceeds customers' expectations; it innovates, expects change as part of the process and takes appropriate risks.* The values and ideals of Zarcone set the climate for a shared vision, which is one of the five disciplines of learning organizations (Senge 1990). Employees want to pursue lofty goals when genuine commitment is fostered to the goals, values, and missions of the organization, and principles and guiding practices enable individual vision to become shared vision.

HDFS is a strong values-based company whose mission is to provide expert financial services for the customers of the Harley-Davidson Motor Company in the best possible way, and their core operating philosophies dovetail with some of the values of the Motor Company.

HDFS has five operating philosophies:

- Customer focus—placing the interests of customers first and seeking to build strong, long-term relationships;
- Investing in employees—cultivating a learning organization where employees enjoy work and receive training, recognition, and opportunity for advancement;
- Honesty and integrity—being truthful and fair, doing the right thing in business dealings and treating each other with mutual respect;
- Commitment to excellence—everyone is responsible for delivering products and services that exceed customers' expectations;
- Entrepreneurial spirit—fostering and rewarding creativity, prudent risk-tasking and a "can do" spirit.

It is easy to see how these core philosophies support a learning organizational culture that is reinforced throughout HDFS by specific leadership actions (Schein 1985). Zarcone, a big proponent of education, notes that *everybody gets at least 24 hours of continuing education training a year.* Furthermore, *we're always trying to figure out new ways to do things; we test new methods, and we make things happen as opposed to standing still.*

Although Zarcone clearly revels in the role of leadership, one trait she does not admire in leaders is when their ego gets in the way. She believes that organizations get into trouble when the personality is so dominant that it is tied to the person as opposed to the leadership team. Teamwork is essential to Zarcone—she has established her own Executive Leadership Team, about 15 people who meet monthly and who in turn meet with their teams and so on so that everyone in the company—750 in total—feels part of the business. *I'm real big on teams,* Zarcone notes, and indeed team learning, one of the five disciplines of learning organizations, is absolutely critical "because teams, not individuals, are the fundamental learning unit in organizations...unless teams can learn, the organization cannot learn" (Senge 1990, 10).

HDFS publishes regular employee newsletters and twice a year, Zarcone holds Town Hall meetings with all the employees, bringing them up-to-date on the company's latest initiatives. Communication is not just one-way however. Staff can either submit questions ahead of time or raise questions during the meetings, and Zarcone answers their questions, which are then posted on the HDFS intranet. True to learning organizations, Zarcone has *worked very hard on changing the culture so people are willing to raise their hand and say there's a problem, and willing to raise it up early so we can get at the problem and find a solution quickly.* Recognizing the importance of secondary reinforcing mechanisms for supporting the culture (Schein 1985), Zarcone holds employee recognition programs during her Town Hall presentations and takes the winners out for dinner.

Zarcone also does a lot of walking around, catching up with staff she has known for years, and introducing herself to new employees. *I try really hard not to be isolated because you get a whole different perspective when you're out and about.* It also gives her an opportunity to relay feedback from customers to her employees.

> *It's a way to stay connected and also get a feel for what's happening. I work with customers quite a bit so I have a sense of how our employees are doing and I make sure I'm carrying the needs of the customer back into the organization. We get feedback regularly from our customers that we're doing the right thing, that they enjoy working with our employees, and that they appreciate the service we are providing. So I let our employees know what we've heard. The positive feedback confirms that we have created a good organization with employees who contribute and make a difference. That's very rewarding... developing what I believe to be a very fine company.*

HDFS is constantly striving to improve and definitely does not stand still. Along with regular feedback from customers, employee surveys are carried out on an ongoing basis and Zarcone is proud that the level of satisfaction from her employee group is extraordinarily high; so the satisfaction of growing a company that is meeting customers' needs gives her a real sense of achievement.

Zarcone most definitely stands behind her employees, and the community in which they work. Just recently, she had to review HDFS's operations in Carson City, Nevada where the company has a major call center with over 450 employees. As the largest private employer in the town, HDFS is an important contributor to the local community. The company had had rental offices in the town for the last ten years and had to decide whether to build a dedicated call center or find an alternative venue for the call center operation elsewhere, possibly overseas. It was a major project to look at all the options and decide what would work best for HDFS in the long run. Zarcone tells the story

Did it make sense to move the call center operation someplace where they are not familiar with Harley-Davidson? One of the things we do differently in our call center is we encourage our staff to stay on the phone and, if the customer wants to talk about their latest ride to Daytona or wherever, we want to hear about it. We want to know what color their motorcycle is or how long they have been riding Harleys, because it's the relationship that we have with our customers that differentiates us. So along with our quantitative analysis, we went through a significant qualitative assessment of our employees, recognizing that their dedication and passion would be difficult to replicate someplace else. Also, we asked ourselves, what was our commitment to them and what was our obligation to them? Our employees are one of our stakeholders and so it's not all just about the bottom line. We believe particularly in the service business that if you have employees who are dedicated, committed and happy, that will come through to the customer. In the end, we decided to invest in our employees and built a cost-effective call center, incorporating increased operational efficiency so that economically it was the smart thing to do for the business. It's been a hugely motivational decision for our employees because they've watched the call center go up, as it was built right across the parking lot from our leased offices.

CONTINUOUS LEARNING IN THE FUTURE

Although she is clearly passionate about her job, Zarcone is also careful to balance her work and personal life—being a wife and the mother of three boys, she is intent on keeping her priorities straight and doesn't lose sight of what is really important. Still, she is able to commit to her future leadership goals.

What else is there for Zarcone to achieve? She admits that she really doesn't know exactly what she wants to do next, but she occasionally yearns to return to her entrepreneurial roots. However, she is very proud of what she has accomplished so far and has many more years and opportunities ahead of her yet! The company continues to show strength, and recently HDFS received the 2004 Catalyst Award which recognizes companies with strong initiatives to advance women in business. Twenty-nine percent of HDFS's corporate officers are women compared to the Fortune 500 average of 16%—an amazing statistic in light of the fact that the majority of Harley-Davidson customers are male! And equally impressive, two of the top five earners in the company are women. Rightly so, Zarcone is very proud of Harley-Davidson's record when it comes to promoting women in the workplace.

Zarcone is all about learning, growth, and development for her organization and herself as a leader. In early 2005, she joined the board of CIGNA Corporation, a health care and insurance company in the top Fortune 150 and she is delighted to report that it is a good company for women. She was the fourth woman on the board (now three as one woman director left to become the U.S. Ambassador to Finland), and she is confident that it ranks among the top of U.S. public companies with the highest percentage of women on their boards. CIGNA has also been consistently in the media as a great place for women to work. As she says, *I'm looking forward to being able to help more women as a mentor and as a leader. Hopefully I can be an influencer to increase the number of talented and highly qualified women in leadership roles. This is my first corporate board outside of HDFS; I've been on a number of non-profit boards.* Recognizing the impact of continuous learning to her ongoing development as a leader, Zarcone continues to take seminars and courses today, because *I find there are areas in which I need to grow. I think I'll continue not only to see how I can help this organization grow, but also how I can grow personally and continue to learn and make a difference.*

REFERENCES

Schein, E. 1985. *Organizational culture and leadership.* San Francisco: Jossey-Bass.
Senge, P. 1990. *The fifth discipline: The art & practice of the learning organization.* New York: Doubleday.

Conclusion: Emergent Themes in Women's Leadership

In our efforts to identify an extraordinary group of women leaders who have achieved success in their business organizations, whether those institutions were corporate, union-based, or entrepreneurial, our primary areas of interest were in each woman's path to success. We studied how women leaders attend to the organizational culture, whether and how they consciously create and maintain it, and by what methods. We also looked at women entrepreneurs who take on the tasks of building businesses at the same time as they are carving out nontraditional career paths. Perhaps most importantly, we focused on the many leadership styles that women utilize to create success for themselves and their organizations. Recognizing that there are many effective styles of leadership, we wanted to learn what was unique about each woman. At the same time, we found that there were also characteristics and approaches that these women shared. The following content summary extracts what we found to be the more common characteristics and behaviors across the women leaders that we interviewed.

The three main areas of focus in each interview were

- Basic demographic and background information, especially noting any role models and mentors and how each woman got to where she is today;
- Personal values, as well as the values of the organization, and how they are linked to each woman's creation and maintenance of organizational culture; and
- Leadership style and what makes each woman unique as a leader. This may include decision-making style and views on ethics.

The specific topics addressed in the interviews included

- How each woman's background prepared her for leadership positions;
- Issues faced as a leader;
- Leadership style and values;
- The culture of the organization; and
- Opportunities and challenges for women leaders.

DEMOGRAPHIC AND BACKGROUND INFORMATION

The women interviewed represented a diverse set of industries, including accounting, aerospace, architecture and design, consulting, education, energy, executive search, financial services, food and beverage, government, health care, manufacturing, public relations, real estate, shipping, and venture capital. Of the industries represented, over three-quarters of our interviewees classified their industries as being "male-dominated." Five percent described them as "female-dominated," and 18% did not specify.

The size of the organizations represented in this study varied greatly, reflecting the diversity of organizations led by women executives today. Company size varied from small businesses to large corporations. Sixty-eight percent of the women noted that their organizations were "industry leaders" or "top performers."

The titles of the women leaders at the time of the interviews were broken down into the following categories:

59%	Owner/Founder/CEO/President
18%	Executive VP/Senior VP/VP
9%	Managing Director
5%	Retired
9%	Not specified

Many of the women interviewed were the founders of their own organizations, including Phyllis Apelbaum, Ellen Carnahan, Adela Cepeda, Alison Chung, Caroline Sanchez Crozier, Mary Ann Leeper, Madeleine Ludlow, Eva Maddox, Barbara Provus, and Donna Zarcone. Of these, only one, Eva Maddox, has sold her company to a larger organization.

Although we strived for diversity in our sample, the reality is that the number of women of color who serve as directors and executive officers is still below an acceptable standard. Of fifty Chicago companies studied by The Chicago Network in their annual census report, in 2006, just 3.9% of all directors were women of color and 1.9% of top executive officers were women of color. However, these statistics have improved from 2005, up from 2.8% and 1.4%, respectively (The Chicago Network 2006). Of the twenty-two women interviewed, seventeen are Caucasian, two are African-American, two are Hispanic, and one is Asian-American.

Many of these women are on the move both within their existing organizations and also between organizations, with the majority of participants having served in their current positions for less than five years. As one reads in the Appendix, ten of the women we interviewed have since changed organizations or started new enterprises. These women may represent a cadre of "new age" managers and executives who give their undivided attention and focus to their work, but who may change the setting of that commitment.

New age managers see themselves as well-trained professionals, not as employees and not as permanently committed to one company or firm (Werhane and Radin 2003). Many of these are uncompromising in their integrity and work ethic, but their loyalties are first to professional integrity, to their clients, and to their fellow-workers, and only secondarily to the particular company with which they are associated. They often change jobs or form new organizations many times while advancing their careers. Furthermore, as noted by Werhane and Radin (2003), such women and men often become leaders in their field, but not necessarily in the same company with which they began their career. This breed of executive is well prepared for the twenty-first century where job security and lifetime employment are no longer viable options, if they ever were.

SHARED LEADERSHIP STYLES

Many of the women included in this book are models of a transformational leadership style. Unlike leaders in hierarchically structured organizations, these women do not view their authority as a matter of power, nor do they think of themselves as persons in superior positions of formal authority. These women are not transactional leaders who view leadership as a series of transactions between managers and employees, a trade of promotion or salary for good performance, or a "punishment" of demotion or firing for poor performance. Rather, they see leadership as an ongoing give-and-take, two-way process where the leader functions in an inspirational rather than directive role. Part of transformational leadership is developing "buy-in" from employees. This leadership style is characterized by shared visioning, which enables leaders as well as followers to establish the values and goals of the company together. This is usually translated into forms of interactive and participatory leadership that empowers employees while achieving corporate ends (Couto 1994). The leadership processes emphasized by the women are participatory and coaching, rather than directing and authoritarian.

Many speak of adding value in their organizations through a participatory, inclusive style of leading their employees as colleagues rather than as subordinates or followers. Indeed, the terms "subordinate" and "follower" seldom surfaced in the interviews we conducted. We were struck with how important the participatory style is to most of the leaders in our study. We were also interested in how each woman interacted with her subordinates, or employees. Many women identified communication and accessibility as key ingredients to a successful relationship. Open and direct communication with both employees and clients was stressed as a critical success factor for maintaining positive relationships. Being approachable to others and being respected were also important characteristics to the women studied.

WISDOM AND SELF-CONFIDENCE

In his book, *Leading Minds*, Howard Gardner argues that two conditions for leadership in any venue are intelligence, what he calls "the attainment of expertise in various domains," and a strong "sense of self" which manifests itself in leaders as self-confidence (Gardner and Laskin 1995, 29). Most of the women we studied were highly educated. Eight of the twenty-two women hold Masters of Business degrees, two hold Juris Doctorate degrees, and one has her Ph.D. Of the other half of our interviewees, the majority has their bachelors degree and three have various masters degrees. The diversity in responses to this question demonstrates that academic achievement is not necessarily a prerequisite for reaching the highest echelons of an organization, or for predicting leadership potential. Most of the women interviewed said that their educational experiences gave them an opportunity to socialize and grow. Many cited the importance of making these experiences a life-long learning process. Despite various struggles and challenges and even discriminatory treatment, each has achieved success in the workplace.

MOTIVATION TO LEAD

A major motivating factor for the women leaders was to ensure financial security for their families. Seventy-three percent of leaders' principal motivating factors were personal growth and professional growth. Others mentioned belief in the company mission, providing products and services highly essential and beneficial to the general public. Some of the leaders were motivated by their ethical values as well as the need to establish a good quality of work life for employees.

WORK/LIFE BALANCE AND OTHER OBSTACLES

Some of the women entrepreneurs cited access to capital as their main obstacle. Some of the women mentioned the challenge of work/life balance. Ten percent of leaders faced personal obstacles such as health problems. Eighteen percent reported obstacles with keeping the work/family balance. Twenty-three percent reported obstacles with being discriminated as a woman leader in their industry. Forty-one percent reported professional obstacles such as adjusting their leadership style, being new to the company or the industry. Only a few participants felt they didn't have any or had only some minor obstacles.

Is it possible that many of these women had a strong "survive and thrive" mentality that drove them to become successful? What does this "survive and thrive" mentality have to do with leadership? Having to survive in difficult environments or under stress or because of tragedy is one of many mechanisms that can push potential leaders into leadership positions. This does not imply that all those in such situations will become leaders. Such challenges, however, are prods and set the stage for those who are capable to become leaders.

ROLE MODELS AND MENTORS

During the interviews we asked each woman about her personal role models and mentors. We delineated these influences by describing a role model as a person who serves as a model in a particular behavioral or social role, and a mentor as a trusted counselor or advisor in an occupational or professional setting. However, during the interviews the leaders often blurred the line between these influences.

Role models played an important part in many of the women's development as a leader. Fifty-nine percent of the women named a family member as her role model—her mother, father, aunt, or even grandparents. Twenty-seven percent reported having professional role models such as a previous manager or partner. Five percent remember their role models from school or sports.

Almost half of the women interviewed reported that their professional mentor was either the person who worked in the position before she took over or someone else in the industry. Women named both women and men as mentors; however, men were mentioned more often than women, underscoring the need to share stories such as these to inspire the women leaders of the future. At least one woman, Donni Case, reported that her so-called organizational mentors were in fact negative role models. She found that many of the managers and executives to whom she reported became negative mentors. They not only did not help her, they discouraged her progress and demeaned her as a woman. Rather than becoming discouraged, however, she used the negative mentoring she received as data for ways *not* to manage and lead. Thus, she turned what, for most women, are negative experiences that become detrimental to their careers into learning experiences from which she could develop her own leadership style as antithetical to that of these non-mentors.

The majority of the women stated that they try to be a mentor to others. The manifestation of this role varied with women mentoring others in their families, their communities, as well as in their workplaces, both formally and informally. When we suggested to each of the women that they were role models to professional women everywhere, many demurred. They seemed very humble about the impact they may have on others as role

when we asked the leaders about what others may notice
...odels, many of the women agreed on the importance of
...airness, approachability, confidence, commitment (follow-
...d being a team player.

PE... AND ORGANIZATIONAL VALUES

One leadership challenge in today's changing business environment involves integrating one's personal values in a competitive arena where ethical issues seem not to be part of everyday business. An important factor affecting managerial decision-making is how managers and professionals prioritize personal, client, corporate, and professional responsibilities. The dilemma of which should take precedence and the misalignment of these personal and organizational values are well illustrated in the number of corporate scandals we have witnessed in the past five years.

Not every organization associated with our study had a formal vision or mission statement, but most of the women leaders reported that their values were closely aligned with those of their organization and were highly consistent with the company culture. The personal values mentioned most often were integrity, transparency, truthfulness, hard work, and commitment—both to the company and to employees or colleagues. Specifically, for fifty-five percent of leaders values such as justice, integrity, high ethics, and truthfulness are the most important. Twenty-three percent believe that family/religious values are the most important. Fourteen percent of the leaders find professional and innovative values are imperative for their work. Moreover, these values spilled over to clients and in decisions as to which business opportunities to undertake or reject. For many of the women, their personal values were closely aligned with the corporate culture that they strived to instill, and many highlighted the importance of their employees having a clear sense of right and wrong.

What is the difference between ethical leadership and a values-based view? Values-based leaders create or propound values for their instrumental worth to create social responsibility, and they align employees and shareholders to accept and work for those values. An ethical leader continually tests these values against societal norms, organizational consistency, and outcomes (Freeman et al. 2006), and instills them in the corporate culture. Social responsibility is one of the six drivers of corporate reputation (Reputation Institute 2007), which is increasingly being recognized as a corporate asset. Companies stand to gain sales, among other outcomes, when their corporate reputation is high (Harris Interactive 2007). Many leaders in the study are explicitly values-based leaders, especially in those companies such as ShoreBank, the Female Health Company, and CSC Learning that have a social as well as financial mission. Almost every woman felt a social responsibility to her community. Almost all found time to give back to the community in one way or another, despite their limited free time. Some have helped to found community service organizations, others volunteer on community boards. The women also serve as coaches, teachers, or volunteers for Little League, religious organizations, mentoring programs, and summer camps.

ON POWER AND INFLUENCE

When asked whether they were motivated by the desire for power or influence in their careers, as many as half of the women acknowledged that they possessed power and that it was important for their roles. However, many of the women said that they do not like the term "power" and prefer the idea of influencing and leading others as an alternative. A few women felt that credibility and strong values were more important leadership characteristics than influence or power.

GREATEST ACCOMPLISHMENT AND THE IDEAL ORGANIZATION

The greatest accomplishment shared by each woman leader was very different. The accomplishment that was most often mentioned was making a profit. Other successes noted included the firm's survival in the industry, organizational or culture change, providing competitive compensation for employees, making a social contribution, and receiving recognition in the industry. Many of the women we studied in this sample seemed to care more about the sustained success of their organization than their own legacy. Jim Collins sees that as a trait he calls Level 5 Leadership, where the future of the organization preempts personal glory. Such leaders realize that the best organization is one that can be great without them (Collins 2001).

Women were asked to complete the sentence, "The ideal organization...." Many responses discussed the importance of bringing out the best in employees. Other responses included having stable financials, a culture based on respect, and a willingness to listen to employees. An organization that values ethics was also important. Some answered that the ideal organization is driven by performance, one that maintains and promotes values, and one that values the well-being of its employees.

Finally, each of the women was asked about her goals for the future. The most common response was to expand and grow their company. Some women mentioned personal goals and passing down their legacy. Other women were looking to explore new avenues for their current business models and create a strong organizational culture. Still others saw themselves as explorers on new paths of discovery yet to be realized.

CONCLUDING THOUGHTS: WOMEN LEADERS IN THE TWENTY-FIRST CENTURY

The qualitative data gathered from the twenty-two interviews in this book do not provide a point-by-point road map of how to become a woman leader in the corporate or entrepreneurial arena. Instead, each woman's story serves as a stepping-stone, moving us forward to a better understanding of how to bolster, support, and promote women executives in the future. The similarities in the paths these women have forged, coupled with the diverse experiences that each woman shares, serve as a compass to point us in the right direction—toward a new world of women leaders in business who shape organizations and communities.

Real leaders always take the risk of helping somebody along who is potentially going to supplant them. But that is what it is all about. You cannot lead forever, you cannot live forever.

—Donni Case

REFERENCES

Collins, James. 2001. Level 5 leadership: The triumph of humility and fierce resolve. *Harvard Business Review* 79 (1): 67–76.

Couto, Richard A. 1994. The transformation of transforming leadership. In *Leader's companion*, ed. J. Thomas Wren, 102–7. New York: Free Press.

Freeman, R.E., K. Martin, B. Parmar, M. Cording, and P.H. Werhane. 2006. Leading through values and ethical principles. In *Inspired leaders,* ed. R. Burke and C. Cooper, 149–74. London: Routledge Taylor and Francis Group.

Gardner, Howard, and Emma Laskin. 1995. *Leading minds.* New York: Basic Books.

Harris Interactive. 2007. *Corporate reputation.* Retrieved March 21, 2007. http://www.harrisinteractive.com/services/reputation.asp.

Reputation Institute. 2007. *Corporate reputation quotient.* Retrieved March 21, 2007. http://www.valuebasedmanagement.net/methods_corporate_reputation_quotient.html.

The Chicago Network. 2006. *The Chicago network 2006 census: Action required.* The Chicago Network Annual, 11.

Werhane, Patricia, and Tara J. Radin with Norman Bowie. 2003. *Employment and employee rights.* Boston, MA: Basil Blackwell.

Appendix

INTERVIEW METHODOLOGY

The material presented in this book is the result of twenty-two interviews conducted with women leaders in both corporate and entrepreneurial enterprises. Most of the women interviewed are members of The Chicago Network, an organization of professional women in the Chicago metropolitan area who have reached the highest echelons of business, the arts, government, the professions, and academia. The remaining women are personal contacts of one or more of the authors. The sample can be regarded as one of convenience; however, the interviewees represented a diverse group of women leaders with respect to industry, position, years of service, ownership vs. managerial status, and personal background.

The interviews were conducted in a verbal format. At the end of the interview each woman completed a short, written demographic survey. The interviews were generally recorded and then transcribed to maintain the unique voice of each interviewee. Once all of the interviews were complete, a content analysis was performed to examine the qualitative data collected and to highlight the themes and issues discovered in the interviews.

INTERVIEW QUESTIONS

The detailed interview format included the following questions:

- Participant's name
- Name of current organization
- What is your current position?

- How many years have you been in your current position?
- Did you actively seek your current position? How did you come to be here?
- What were your principal motivating factors?
- What obstacles did you face?
- Who were your role models?
- Did you have any mentors?
- Do you consider yourself a mentor?
- How do you feel about being a role model? What would you say others notice about you the most?
- Have your educational experiences shaped your development as a leader?
- What do you believe your greatest accomplishment at your organization has been? Briefly describe what that accomplishment was and how it was achieved. Who else, if anyone, was involved in this effort with you? How did you get others "on board" with what you were trying to accomplish? What were the key factors that influenced your decision-making for this accomplishment?
- How do you measure "success" for your actions and your organization?
- How would you describe your personal values?
- How would you describe the values of your organization?
- What is your organization's vision and/or mission statement?
- What are some of your day-to-day actions that embody that vision?
- What have you done to ensure that the vision is carried out by your organization?
- What obstacles do you face within your organization to carry out your leadership goals?
- How do you interact with your followers or subordinates?
- Have you experienced any ethical dilemmas in your leadership role? Could you provide an example? How did you handle it? Did it change the way you lead?
- How important was the desire for power or influence in motivating you to higher positions in your career?
- Please fill in the blank. The ideal organization....
- What goals do you have for your future?

DEMOGRAPHIC QUESTIONNAIRE

The following demographic information was also collected for each woman:

- Participant's Name
- Industry
- Male- or Female-Dominated Industry
- Name of Current Organization
- Size of Current Organization
- Position of Organization in the Industry (i.e., industry leader, place on Fortune 500, etc.)
- Current Position
- Years in Current Position
- Years of Education
- Highest Level of Education Achieved
- Race
- Age
- Marital Status
- Number and Ages of Children

WOMEN LEADERS PROFILED

The following list represents the women interviewed for this book. Next to each woman's name we have listed her position at the time of the interview, as well as a new position, if applicable.

Phyllis Apelbaum, President and CEO, Arrow Messenger Service, Inc.
Anne L. Arvia, formerly President and CEO, Shorebank; President and CEO, Nationwide Bank
Margaret Blackshere, Retired President, Illinois AFL-CIO
Gail Boudreax, Executive Vice President, External Operations, Health Care Service Corporation
Cathy Calhoun, President, Weber Shandwick-Chicago; Co-President, Global Consumer Marketing
Ellen Carnahan, formerly Managing Director, William Blair Capital Partners; Cofounder and Managing Director, Seyen Capital
Donni Case, former President, Financial Relations Board; Chair, Vistage International
Adela Cepeda, President and CEO, A.C. Advisory, Inc.; CEO, Alta Capital Group LLC
Alison Chung, President, TeamWerks
Caroline Sanchez Crozier, Founder, CEO and President, CSC Learning
Deborah L. DeHaas, Vice Chairman and Midwest Regional Managing Partner, Deloitte & Touche USA LLP
Sondra Healy, Co-Chairman, Turtle Wax
Dr. Mary Ann Leeper, Senior Strategic Advisor, Female Health Company

Madeleine W. Ludlow, Chairman of the Board and former CEO, Cadence Network Inc.; Founder and Principal, LudlowWard Capital Advisors

Eva Maddox, Design Principal, Perkins+Will / Eva Maddox Branded Environments

Beth Prichard, CEO and President, Dean & DeLuca

Barbara L. Provus, Retired Principal and Founder, Shepherd, Bueschel & Provus, Inc.; Board Member, The Anti-Cruelty Society, The Chicago Network

Martha Ries, Vice President, Ethics & Business Conduct, The Boeing Company

Desiree Rogers, President, Peoples Gas and North Shore Gas, the Illinois utilities of Integrys Corporation

Paula A. Sneed, Retired Executive Vice President, Global Marketing Resources & Initiatives, Kraft Foods, Inc.; Board of Directors for Airgas, Inc., Charles Schwab Corporation, and Tyco Electronics, Inc.

Pamela Strobel, Retired Executive Vice President and CAO, Exelon; Director of State Farm Mutual Automotive Insurance Company and Domtar Corporation

Donna F. Zarcone, formerly President and COO of Harley-Davidson Financial Services; President and CEO, D.F. Zarcone & Associates LLC

Index

About the Authors

LISA GUNDRY is Professor of Management in the Charles H. Kellstadt Graduate School of Business at DePaul University, where she teaches courses in creativity and innovation in business and entrepreneurship. She is the coauthor of five books and has published numerous journal articles and book chapters.

LAUREL OFSTEIN is an Instructor in the Department of Management at the Charles H. Kellstadt Graduate School of Business at DePaul University, where she teaches courses in business creativity and entrepreneurship.

MARGARET POSIG is an Associate Professor of Management in the Charles H. Kellstadt Graduate School of Business at DePaul University. Her articles have appeared in the *Journal of Occupational Health Psychology, Women in Management Review, Journal of Managerial Issues,* and *Journal of Business Ethics,* among others. She teaches courses in organizational leadership and change management, and leadership in sports.

ELIZABETH POWELL is an Assistant Professor of Business Administration at the Darden Graduate School of Business Administration at the University of Virginia. The author of several case studies, she has presented her research at the Conference on Corporate Communication, the Management Communication Association, and the National Communication Association.

PATRICIA WERHANE is the Wicklander Chair of Business Ethics and Director of the Institute for Business and Professional Ethics at DePaul University. She holds a joint appointment as the Peter and Adeline Ruffin Professor of Business Ethics and Senior Fellow at the Olsson Center for Applied Ethics at the Darden School, University of Virginia. She is the author or editor of twenty-two books and the founder and former editor in chief of *Business Ethics Quarterly.*